Knowledge and practical knowledge

Work & Society

Vol. 88

Silvia CARBONE

Knowledge and practical knowledge

For an analysis of the working practices of social workers

PETER LANG

Bruxelles - Berlin - Chennai - Lausanne - New York - Oxford

Il presente volume è stato pubblicato con il contributo straodinario dell'Università degli Studi di Messina

© 2024 Peter Lang Group AG, Lausanne

Published by Peter Lang Éditions Scientifiques Internationales - P.I.E. SA, Brussels, Belgium
info@peterlang.com - www.peterlang.com

ISSN 1376-0955
ISBN 978-3-0343-4930-7
ePDF 978-3-0343-4931-4
ePub 978-3-0343-4932-1
DOI 10.3726/b21787
D/2024/5678/46

Bibliographic information published by the Deutsche Nationalbibliothek. The German National Library lists this publication in the German National Bibliography; detailed bibliographic data is available on the Internet at http://dnb.d-nb.de.

Il presente volume è stato pubblicato, in parte, con il contributo straodinario dell'Università degli Studi di Messina

For all my students,

young and old,

from whom I have learned a lot.

Table of contents

Introduction 13
    Themes and objectives of the research 13
    The path, method and techniques 15

Chapter 1 The institutional, historical and cultural dimensions of the social worker 19
    1.1 Historical background 19
    1.2 The new coming of age 21

Chapter 2 The dynamic analysis of the profession of social workers 25
    2.1 Macro approach 25
    2.2 Micro approach 27
    2.3 Interactionism 31

Chapter 3 The daily work of the social worker 35
    3.1 Working between relationship and articulation 37
    3.2 Situated activity to practical knowledge 44
    3.3 Work practices 46

Chapter 4 Body-mediated knowledge 51
    4.1 Body and practical knowledge 51
    4.2 Tacit knowledge 54
    4.3 Bodies at work 56

Chapter 5 The discursive practice of the social worker 59
    5.1 Communicative competence 59
    5.2 Mimetic conversations 65

5.3 Understanding words 67
5.4 Using words in writing 71
5.5 Narrative 73

Chapter 6 Social workers and the reception of refugees/asylum seekers: Institutional coordination and cooperation .. 77

6.1 National reception policy framework 77
6.2 SWOT Analysis 79
6.3 Attention to cooperation 86
6.4 Communication between parties 88

Considerations 91

Bibliography 95

Introduction

Themes and objectives of the research

Sociology has considered work as situated activity due to the thrust, which other disciplines such as ethnomethodology, have had to face with respect to certain issues that have emerged especially from contemporary society labeled as a society of knowledge and practical knowledge. The work practice of the social worker constitutes a unit of analysis proposed in this book for the study of this work practice, understood as situated activity. The value of work, theoretical tools and methods for looking at work as a practical cognitive activity are still in a stage of reflection. But how to empirically study the practical knowledge of social workers? The objective of this book is to explore the way in which the work practice of social workers is expressed in a local contest Messina. The research was divided into related questions:

(a) how the work activity of social workers takes shape in terms of individuals and the internal organization of the structure;
(b) how the relationship between knowledge and practical knowledge affects professional vision, performance and the choices of action to be taken.

Let us start with a delimitation of the phenomenon we are interested in circumscribing: knowledge as a practical activity. We will then go on to address a methodology for analyzing work as knowledge work under the assumption that all activities, whether individual or collective, incorporate elements that give them a collective, that is, social, character. They are mediated by the body, language and objects anchored in the social dimension, responding to the activity of others and soliciting them. They are material and discursive practices. On the other hand, activities are concretely inscribed in social organization by means of collectives that help structure them through the definition of roles. Working therefore is a knowing how to do in situations, a knowing how to work together, weaving relationships between people, between other professionals and objects, languages, technologies and institutions. All these things, found in the social worker's field of action, are partly given, partly to be sought, and partly missing, and must be brought together within a network that connects them in a meaningful way, that makes them together go together. This image recalls the activity of bricolage rather than that of planning. For this we will use concepts such as articulation work, relationship work, arbitrage, alignment. To give the idea that resources for action (material, communicative, etc.), must be activated and put into reaction in order to maintain a common orientation.

In particular, a specific finding that we believe is original to this investigation concerns an in-depth analysis of the work practice of social workers in services, in a local contest (Messina), oriented toward the reception of refugees and asylum seekers, as a process in which they bring to the table their practical knowledge necessary to carry out their work, including through coordination with other institutions.

To do so, we must start with some basic assumptions, salient to our research, which refer back to established findings in the international literature:

- Work is a practical activity constructed by both the social worker and the person, within situations and interactions that take place predominantly face-to-face, and therefore need to be studied in situ;
- Cooperation, with the rest of the team, is the result of continual adjustment to unforeseen events that emerge from the context;
- Human activity in situation does not follow absolute rationality, as those involved in a work practice constantly give rise to reciprocal actions and interactions, so a reflexive attitude that recognizes the partiality of any source of knowledge is necessary.

The profession of social work can find itself caught between the enterprise of governing uncertainty or being overwhelmed by it, and the risk of becoming alternately insecure or conversely overly rigid. While uncertainty urges the need for constant research and new construction of knowledge, all forms of knowledge cannot be thought of as mechanical. The social worker moves on uncertain and ambiguous terrain, and in this sense is an inherently research profession, but the intertwining of research and practice requires processes of reflection and thinking (Fargion, 2013). As Schon (1983) would say, some professionals, among whom we include social workers, do not face well-defined situations. In this case, the professional's task would be to classify the problem, relate it to theoretical categories, and finally find the best solution paths. Among the findings of this book, there certainly emerges a clear understanding that the essence of a social worker's work is to create an interaction with people who often experience a magmatic, undefined, fluctuating situation. This interaction has to be built through a dialogue based on the ability to interrogate situations, to ask questions and study ways to deal with them. It is a dialogue that is developed through a confrontation with different knowledge (psychologists, civil servants, etc.) and that leads to the production of more possible scenarios and ways to deal with the situation. The social worker cannot call himself or herself out of whatever scenario he or she constructs; in fact, he or she must be aware that the moment he or she produces an interpretation of reality he or she is already acting on it and modifying it. On this basis we have built this second step of the research, the methodological choices and operational steps of which we are going to outline.

The path, method and techniques

It began with making contacts, thanks to the FAMI-ARES project, which covered the training of operators and social workers working in Third Sector associations and cooperatives involved in the reception of refugees/asylum seekers on behalf of the Prefecture of Messina. Through these moments, conducted within the University of Messina from June 2022 to July 2023: 15 social workers, 2 educators, 1 social operator, 1 mediator, 1 trainee social worker were interviewed (Table 6.1). In Sicily, the constantly increasing flow of asylum seekers and refugees by sea and by land was perceived as an emergency which led to an extraordinary management of reception. The arrival of asylum-seeking migrants in Sicily, especially in Messina, has made it difficult to reorganize the social service and the working practice of social workers employed in the reception of migrants. Social workers have great potential to be activated before/during/and after the settlement of asylum seekers if they manage to be aware of the historical present and of the challenges posed by the current economic, demographic and political situation. Managing reception policies in terms social service means acting at the level of a public organization which is always characterized by the collaboration implemented with other professionals and actors from the public, private and voluntary sectors. Within the theoretical and methodological framework used in this book to analyze the work practice of social workers as practical knowledge, taking into account the relationship that binds knowledge to practical knowledge, we can consider this knowledge an activity to be studied as a situated activity, that is, a contextual knowledge, anchored in the context of its production, in this case refugee/asylum seeker services.

The subject matter to be investigated, and the weight assumed by the subjectivity involved, has led to a preference, in accordance with the principles of grounded theory (Glaser and Strauss, 1967), for tools of qualitative analysis. This allowed a theoretical formulation from data possible through the connection between research and practice, following the Practice Research (PR) approach. At the core of the research is the idea of studying the experiences of those involved, and building knowledge from the so-called practical wisdom, the expertise gained from those who experience problems directly. The consolidation over the past two decades of the PR strand of social studies based on practical knowledge has resulted in knowledge being qualified as practical. Professions, according to this perspective, should not be framed descriptively, but interpreted as categories that are part of everyday life. Attracting attention, therefore, are all those micro sociological behaviors and processes that, in analyzing the encounter between knowledge and practical knowledge, consider work as a situated activity capable of generating, by working, further knowledge. Studying the work of the social worker as practical knowledge and situated activity is constituted with the intention of replacing objective rationality (decontextualized rationality) with the logic of the situation (contextual rationality). The proposal of this text also rests on this awareness, namely, that of enriching the research process, and adopting a micro-sociological approach, which, mingling with practical knowledge, can bring to light hitherto unexplored insights and evidence on how social workers construct their knowledge and decline their profession, in a continuous process of interaction and reflection.

The interviews and workshops were conducted by the writer. Following this approach, it was possible to investigate not only the representations partials of social workers, but the complex structuring of their work practice. The study of these analyzed cases and the processing of the responses, made it possible to draw sound insights for reflection. It should be remembered that the aim of the research, was not so much to test hypotheses, but to analyze and explicate the working practice of social workers, in order to add more general awarenesses in the ways of professional action. It can be seen that the overall set of interviewees, the resulting body of information, is the result of a selective and self-selective process articulated in several steps: (1) identification of inclusion criteria by the research unit; (2) selection of potential interviewees; and (3) degree of the interviewee's willingness to recount aspects of their profession and training.

As for the type of analysis of the interviews collected, we reflected in order to the classification proposed by Demazière and Dubar (2000). Looking at the landscape of research based on interview analysis, three different attitudes were broadly identified, each of which refers to a certain idea of the relationship between theory and empirical research. The first attitude is called "illustrative" in the sense that it indicates the use of interview texts to illustrate and confirm the theoretical framework constructed by the researcher for his or her investigation. Parts of the interviews in fact are extracted and included in the research in order to exemplify findings of the theoretical construction. The second attitude is the restitutive one, which proceeds in an opposite way to the first, giving maximum priority to the point of view, categories and meanings expressed by the interviewee, which are considered transparent in themselves. The third and last attitude is the analytical one, which in taking the interview text seeks to grasp its perspective of meaning produced by the interviewee and to show its articulation, its structure. The latter attitude, consistent with this research, was more able to achieve a balance between attention to the sense perspective expressed by the interviewee and the theoretical categories constructed by the researcher also on the basis of the literature and previous research, which can guarantee, albeit problematically, a certain objectivity. We therefore coded the interviews according to these three levels of attitudes, then reported within this scheme what seemed to us to be the most relevant segments and which form the object and reconstruction of logic in each interview. The names of the interviewees and places, have been changed to ensure anonymity.

Finally, for the processing of the material that emerged from the workshops and interviews we identified specific miniaturization tools (Bruschi, 1999) that could hold the acquired textual corpus together in an initial summary. It was not easy to govern a textual corpus composed of 20 participants, and to be able to embrace its salient features at a single glance. In the first stage, thematic summaries were used. The thematic summary summarizes in a few lines the contents expressed during the two workshops read mainly in light of the question that inspired this research: (i) the focus on cooperation; (ii) situated knowledge and communication between parties. In a second step, a biographical record was compiled, set taking into account the SWOT scheme, through which the events narrated during the workshops were sorted into a synoptic table describing them, offering for each one three analytical outline information: (a) the educational dimension: years of professional experience; (b) the work dimension: service where the professional activity is carried out; (c) gender. It was thus possible to immediately compare the responses of the 20 participants and, in general, the same text corpus of interest to the research. The combination of these two phases resulted in a matrix containing some quotations from the workshops, which return some fragments in this direction, and through an analysis of the sequences of the lemmas of the interview fragments, taken from the schematization, it was possible to carry out a calculation of the occurrences (most named words) at Figure 6.2 and the co-occurrences present in the interviews (Figure 6.3), through the use of the software T.Lab

The book deals with a very important topic that straddles sociology and social services, and which certainly deserves to be discussed and explored. This book revitalizes micro-social studies of the work of social workers, thereby increasing interdisciplinary cooperation with those involved in social services and social policy. It is important today to ask ourselves: what could be the lines of development and the motivations behind the concept of practical knowledge? Thanks to this book, future research dealing with the work practice of social workers will also have a basis for comparison with other social work. The final chapter of the volume is research based and the results could be important and relevant for national but also international social work community. This would allow for greater comparison and better definition of the analysis conducted in this book.

Chapter 1
The institutional, historical and cultural dimensions of the social worker

1.1. Historical background

The work practice of social workers, however situated it may be, does not take shape in an empty space, but reflects and translates the values and beliefs of a larger professional society and community. One cannot ignore the fact that the work of the social worker enjoys its own specific historicity that makes it different from other types of work. This is to say that a situated analysis of the social worker's work must also be able to take into account what is the institutional, historical and cultural dimension in which this work practice took shape, because there is a linear relationship between the historical evolution of the social worker's work and situated practice. But also because the historical-institutional background is part of the set of elements that mediate and support the work of the social worker. In this sense, it is useful to make a reference on the historical excursus of the social worker's work, in the Italian context. The history of social service locates the birth of the figure of the social worker in the England of the Industrial Revolution, when starting in 1869 London's Charity Organizations Societies (COS) grew up in the territory, with the aim of helping and supporting the poor who were suffering the negative effects of the Industrial Revolution. Social work initially consisted of religious volunteer initiatives, and gradually began to structure ethical principles and methods of intervention that within a few years constituted the subject of teaching in the Schools of Social Service that sprang up in Northern Europe and the US. These operational experiences began to spread in several countries at the end of the 19th century. In Italy, the first Schools of Social Service occur in 1920, and slowly spread to the rest of Italy, although the training was for future "social secretaries," who were primarily to perform the task of supporting workers in factories by mediating with the employer. Despite these early experiences, in fact, studies on the subject (Neve, 2008) agree that the origin of Italian social service dates back to the post-World War II period, beginning with the Tremezzo Convention of 1946, which officially marked the need to reform the welfare system. In the early 1950s, thanks to the influence of the American Schools of Social Service, case work was introduced as the method the social worker had to follow to assess and intervene in social work. It was later replaced by group work and community work. From a training and normative point of view, the work of the social worker is characterized by a very peculiar process of professionalization, as in Italy this figure has experienced an inverse process of institutionalization compared to the typical processes of professional affirmation (such as that of the doctor and lawyer). In fact, the first piece of legislation in which the figure of the social worker is provided for is Law No. 1085/62 on the Ordering of Social Service Offices and Establishment of the Roles of Personnel of the aforementioned service, which in art. 3 provides for the establishment of "a role of managerial personnel and a role of conceptual personnel of the social service." The social worker therefore, starting in the 1960s, began to find a place in public welfare organizations, whereby the development of specific activities and functions differed as the institutional purposes of the various reference bodies changed, increasing more and more functions and tasks. For several decades, the social worker has found employment almost exclusively in public services, translating the professional mandate with the institutional mandate of the reference agency, and identifying as his or her own a multiplicity of practices closely related to the institutional activities of the agencies to which they belong. This has negatively affected the construction of communication codes specific to the profession and shared at the intra-professional and supra-organizational levels. In addition, the absence of an organic law in the care sector has contributed to the persistence of a lack of clarity regarding the role and functions of this professional figure. Institutionally, in 1982 the National Study Commission for the Definition of Professional Profiles and Training Requirements for Social Workers came up with the first official definition of "social worker" in Italy. In 1985, direct university schools for special purposes for social workers were launched and their requirements for access, duration and curriculum were identified, making the training path homogeneous throughout Italy. Law 84/93 established the Professional Order of Social Workers and its Roll, and in

1998 the first Code of Ethics was issued. Finally, with Ministerial Decree 509/1999, the training of social workers is included within the first and second level university courses of study. From the "analysis conducted in recent research (Carbone, 2022) emerges the absence of a clear role specificity and an experience of discomfort in professional practice, but above all the need to focus on professional training, not only the initial one (university/academic), but especially the continuous one referred to the management of increasingly complex problems. As Riva (2009) would say, in fact, the development of social workers" professionalism i2 related to the dissemination of knowledge acquired through training courses. This awareness is more evident in professional social workers who emphasize how training can determine not only the achievement of balance in the concrete relationship with their profession, but also the acquisition and reworking of an awareness, a reflective capacity that is built over time with practical experience.

1.2. The new coming of age

The work of the social worker is a prime example of a job based on practical knowledge, since much of his or her work takes place on the ground and is learned through direct experience. Usually much of this knowledge is passed on from experienced social workers to younger ones through periods of internship and university shadowing. The importance of the university internship is crucial, as students give much attention to their choice of internship (Carbone, 2022). How to prepare for an interview, how to relate to people, how to write the file, how to communicate with other professionals, etc. these are some of the things that junior social workers learn, theoretically in college, and in practice during their internship. Then they have to be able to decline it with respect to their service. During the internship, junior social workers also have a way to observe in action, the professional ethics proper to social workers, and thus realize the institutional dimension of their profession and the social responsibilities it entails. Practical knowledge is imparted by the experienced social worker to the trainee through scaffolding, a metaphor used extensively in the literature by both psychologists and educationalists that indicates the scaffolding that is used in construction to construct a building and then, when the work is completed, is removed (Pontecorvo, Ajello, and Zuccermaglio, 1995). Scaffolding, as a momentary structure, which upon completion of the apprenticeship should be removed, is flexible, that is, adaptable in many different situations, responds to the need to have a support that is sufficiently plastic and removable. As experienced social workers begin to see themselves joined by young trainees, who change frequently, they often teach not only knowledge but also the tricks of the trade. The emerging professional community within social services thus reflects different positions, as these correspond to different ways of working in the day-to-day, as well as interpreting one's role.

As experienced social workers begin to see themselves joined by young trainees, who change frequently, they often teach them more about knowledge, the tricks of the trade. The emerging community of practice within social services thus reflects different positions, as these correspond to different ways of working on a day-to-day basis, as well as of interpreting one's role. An experienced social worker will have a different way of understanding his or her profession than a younger one. Situated work is that collective activity that takes place in a circumscribed place and time, and thus takes on all the dynamism and complexity associated with the context that encloses it and makes it possible. It expresses contextual rationality, that is, a form of action, of practical reasoning, oriented to the object of work, to interactions with others, to the context, and to all the resources within it. In situated terms, what occurs is thus an expansion of knowledge that leads to the evolution of the entire community of practice, with a further reconstruction and enrichment of the historical-institutional dimension of the social worker's work. Starting from work practices thus makes it possible to see how the elements of practical knowledge are of importance to the daily activities of the actors involved, and to overcome the traditional micro-macro dichotomy, in order to incorporate the social context into more complex dynamics of mediation and work accomplishment. The work of the social worker consists of a set of work practices that are repeated daily, adapted to the changing circumstances in which they take place (Dal Pra Ponticelli, 2005). It is this set of work practices, which composes the profession. It consists of working, but how they will be followed and evolve will depend on the specific situation. Work practices can therefore be seen as the unit of analysis of partially given and constantly changing work. They constitute ways of ordering the flow of work, of segmenting it into coherent and interdependent subsets of activities, of codifying it in recognizable and socially recognized and supported ways. For example, arranging an interview or home visit, writing a report, etc. are the basic modes used to order work. They constitute codified situations that contain a program of action, but do not constrain the manner of its execution. Characteristic of the social worker's work practices is therefore not internal variability, but rather its repetition in a practice that tends to evolve, reconstruct itself, innovate. It is such precisely because it is practiced and habitually taught and learned as a basic activity, requiring expert competence. Practices therefore contain elements of habit, but they are not habits. They contain elements of action, but they are not actions in repetition. And these actions are subject to continuous construction and reconstruction rather than sic et simpliciter application of knowledge (López-Pastor, Monjas, and Manrique, 2011). As the defining element of social workers' work practices there is precisely the development of skills. Change, specificity by adaptation to contingencies or by learning, are related in that the daily reproduction of activity engenders an internal dynamic of constant improvement and development. Adaptation, change in view of changed conditions or falling out of use: know-how is refined through being practiced. Learning processes become the symbolic element that motivates doing, rewards it. But what is the relationship between knowledge, knowing and the practice of knowing? Knowledge is not reduced to science, and cannot be regarded as a set of utterances that denote and describe objects. Knowledge is composed of knowledge, but in it converge the ideas of knowing how to live, knowing how to listen. Similarly, we can emphasize the distinction between knowing a practice and knowing in practice. That is, what we have called practical knowledge is different from knowing a practice. An example that we can report here concerns an action-research conducted by third-year (internship) students of the Bachelor of Science in Social Service at the University of Messina, who observed and interviewed some social workers in their working context, that of refugee/asylum-seeker reception centers (Carbone, forthcoming). They were asked to collect field notes, after each observation, in order to share with the researcher, in workshops, relational and contextual elements useful both to the more complete analysis of the interviews made with the social workers who worked in those services, and to reflect with them, in a formative key, of the importance of knowledge in working practice. It was thus possible to highlight possible professional ideal types, but these professional modes are not given once and for all; they are constructed and changed through an ongoing process of interpretation, training and personalization of the profession. What should be emphasized here is that thanks to the workshops with the student trainees involved, it was possible to bring out the tension between knowledge, work situations and professional practical knowledge. On the one hand, the trainees learned, observed and reflected on professional practice, and on the other hand, it was possible to identify and propose to think about his or her practice, observing it closely, in terms of applying models. Gibbons (2011) argues that social work students are often taught professional practice, learning communication and skills. In this regard, he talks about three techniques that might be particularly effective in developing professional practice, namely: mindfulness, experience, and pretence. In the above-mentioned research, we tried to trigger learning through the use of the first two, taking into account that role-playing activities are already carried out in the social service course by the teachers of the professional subjects (principles and fundamentals of social service and methods and techniques of social service). Awareness was achieved through the fieldwork that the trainees themselves did, working alongside the tutor, but especially by reflecting on and analyzing, through direct, up-close experience, the weight of knowledge in work practice. In addition, the shared reading of the trainees' notes from their field observations, cross-referenced with the reading of the interviews done with the social workers, solicited their critical thinking, strengthening their awareness of Self and the profession, in order to hypothesize how it would be possible to govern and transform knowledge into a professional competence. Practical knowledge is thus a knowing *to* operate, where the *to* has an epistemologically constitutive function. It is not already constituted knowledge that applies to operating, but it is knowledge that is constituted as a function of operating. To become a practitioner in this case will say that he or she knows that practice when he or she is able to reproduce it and has been empowered to do so independently having acquired the necessary competence. Thus, there are different types of relationships between practices and practical knowledge: (a) practical knowledge is an activity that takes place within situated practices. In this meaning, practices are containers constituted as objective entities, in that they have been objectified by practitioners who already have knowledge, that is, they recognize them as practices that contain bits of knowledge anchored in the material world; (b) the activities of knowing and practicing are not two separate and detached phenomena, but are mutually constituted; (c) practicing is knowing, through a reproduction and relation of equivalence. In practice whether the subject is aware of it or not, acting as a competent practitioner is synonymous with knowing how to move successfully in the field, performing, that is, expressing that knowledge which is formed in and through the action itself, exceeding knowledge.

Chapter 2
The dynamic analysis of the profession of social workers

The main issues that have attracted the attention of researchers with regard to the study of the social work profession can be summarized in two questions. The first is: how are identities, skills, social roles, professional paths and careers developed? The second is: what are the work practices of social workers? And by what are they determined and influenced? In the first case, the focus is mainly on training and the construction of a professional identity with clear boundaries. In the second case, however, the focus is on work practices, motivations and interactions, and the consequences of these in the relational context in which they take place. The relationship between the two issues also articulates the distinction between professionals within a well-defined organization, and professionals called to perform a specific activity. There is no shortage, however, of perspectives that have attempted to proceed not by exclusionary dichotomies, but rather according to logics of theoretical integration, better able to account for the complexity and interdependencies that characterize care relationships, the bodies that mediate this interaction and their changing dynamics.

2.1. Macro approach

To give an idea of how from different perspectives the work of the social worker is viewed and studied, let us begin by comparing two ways of circumscribing this phenomenon from a sociological perspective. Numerous sociological scholars have dwelt on the concept of the profession and, using different approaches (functionalist, interactionist, Marxist, and neoweberian), have generated wide and diverse contributions, without arriving at a universally accepted definition. Flexner

(1915), was the first to ask the question whether the work of social workers should be considered a true profession. On the one hand, it was possible to find the presence of intellectual training and the provision of community service. On the other, the lack of control among colleagues over individual professional behavior and the existence of an association to evaluate the requirements for entry, did not allow the recognition of the activity of social workers as a profession. Placing the profession of social workers within the Parsonian functionalist interpretive framework was Barber (1963), defining it as emergent or marginal in that it is averagely endowed with a primary orientation toward society and a high level of generalized and systematic knowledge. The functionalist strand later inspired numerous studies conducted specifically on obstacles in the professionalization pathway (Moore, 1970). The functionalist approach, from the early 20th century, saw in Parsons (1939) one of its earliest representatives. He argued that, in the modern era, it was not only individual self-interest that affected professional conduct, but certain institutionalized patterns of reference oriented toward the community. The latter includes Wilensky's (1964) study, which, following empirical research on eighteen American professions, defined social workers as a profession because it has the five stages of the professionalization process: full-time employment; establishment of a training school; creation of a professional association; state support; and creation of a formal code of ethics. Instead, Saunders (1955) called the work of social workers a semi-profession because of the lack of autonomy due to the responsibility that social workers have to the person and the agency. It was Greenwood (1957) who fully recognized its status as a profession, although still developing and inferior to other traditional professions, because it is endowed with: professional skill; professional authority; community sanction; code of ethical rules; and membership in a professional association. This unidirectional sequentiality is reversed by the neo-Weberian approach, which instead tends to analyze professions as organized social groups endowed with: exclusive competence in a given market; control over other occupations; the power to define consumers' needs; and the means of providing for those needs. Among the theorists who represented this current, we may recall Johnson (1972) who viewed occupations as "instruments of control over the relationships" that come into being between the giver of the service (professional) and the user of the professional service (client). Witz's (1992) studies also took up the neo-Weberian strand and, in addition to analyzing professionalization processes from a gender perspective, framed them within the division of labor that takes place within a capitalist system. In this sense, Witz conceived professionalization as a strategy of social closure through which certain occupational groups struggle with each other to increase opportunities and privileges. In the Italian context, on the one hand Prandstraller (1999) emphasized the importance of acquired scientific-technical knowledge as a basic feature of any profession capable of generating new knowledge, practical knowledge; on the other hand Tousijn (1994) conceived the concept of professionalization as consisting of a logical and temporal succession of a series of stages: the formation of a cognitive base; the emergence of local and national professional associations; the rise of specialized schools; and the recognition of forms of state protection. All of which can be interpreted as a professional project directed toward gaining control of the professional market and raising the collective status of members of the profession, although the degree to which the project is realized varies greatly between professions.

2.2. Micro approach

From the theoretical perspectives, previously discussed, the work of the social worker is mainly analyzed through a macro approach. In the 1960s, some Italian sociologists promoted the thesis of social workers as a developing profession. For example, Florea (1966) notes the advance of a professionalization process characterized by a professional commitment that aspires to public recognition. Ferrarotti (1969) recognizes social workers' assumption of a role, behaviors, viewpoints and criteria of judgment that together constitute a specific professional structure. Subsequently, the trend toward the integration of social and health services called for a more qualitative approach aimed at investigating more the new forms of negotiation and professionalism among the different practitioners. According to this view, the dynamics between management and professionalism can lead to five different outcomes: managerial hegemony; co-optation; negotiation; strategic adaptation; and opposition (Numerato et al., 2012). Beginning with the reform of the social welfare system in the 1980s, the attention of scholars on the professional figure of social workers grows again, including Campanini (1999) who highlights the fragility of a figure strongly connected to institutional and social transformations. More recent studies, while not neglecting the strong weight that welfare state transformations have on the profession, have examined its capacity for settling in the public sector on the one hand, and for innovation in the private sector on the other (Ruggeri, 2013). It is on the basis of this complexity that social workers experience in their profession, that some scholars, internationally, such as Dent and Whitehead (2002) found that these professionals find themselves occupying different positions, going through a continuous action of negotiation about their professional identity, which therefore can be considered neither stable nor an end result, but in continuous redefinition. Abbott (1995) also conceived of the work of social workers as a complex profession that must be observed through a systemic lens. In fact, he spoke of a constitutive network approach to examine how social work emerges and differs from other social work. In this regard, it is also important to grasp the contribution of Folgheraiter (1998), who defines social work as a hyperprofession, that is, a profession that in order to be effective and provide concrete answers must combine the practitioner's specific skills with the practitioner's own experiential skills and those that users bring to the counseling relationship. Over the past three decades, analyzes of work activities qualified as "reflective professions" have also gained prominence. This new epistemology of professional practice, based on the distinction between "knowledge in action" and "reflection in the course of action," seeks to understand how professionals deal with those uncertain, peculiar situations steeped in value conflicts that are impossible to resolve by technical knowledge alone. According to Schön (1983), it is the repetition of this reflective practice in the course of action that, transforming into a permanent attitude, generates a true professional identity, giving rise to reflection in action. Archer (2003) beginning with his important conceptual developments concerning the structure-agent problem, related work from analytic dualism, which became known as the morphostatic/morphogenetic approach, also provided influential resources for the critique of post-structuralist and post-modernist thought, and deepened the focus on the nature of human personality and reflexivity in relation to social reality (Archer, 2012). His theories have increased the diversity and nuance of the conceptual components of realism: particularly temporality, culture and the dynamics of reflexivity, and the nature of personality. Through this analytical dualism separating structure and action, it is possible to examine interactions in order to account for the structuring and restructuring of social institutions, that is, in our case, social services. While the latter may be centralized, the human beings working within it are reflexive. Moreover, structure is necessarily prior to the actions that transform it, and, structural processing is necessarily subsequent to those actions. So, technical rationality, based on an applicative and unidirectional view, is strongly challenged, and the result is the enhancement of reflexive practice, of action, as the context in which professionals, as epistemic subjects, learn by doing and in dialogue with the situation in which they work, and restructure structure. Thus, technical rationality, based on an applicative and unidirectional view, is strongly challenged, and the result is the valorization of practice as a context in which professionals, as epistemic subjects, learn by doing and in dialogue with the situation in which they operate. A contribution in this direction, is provided, at the beginning of the new century, by some scholars, who emphasize the importance of the professional ability to combine theoretical knowledge with experiential knowledge, research and practice (Fargion, 2005), in order to create a professional identity based on reflection and thinking. Professions, according to this perspective, should not be framed descriptively, but interpreted as categories that are part of everyday life. Attracting attention, therefore, are all those micro sociological behaviors and processes that, in analyzing the encounter between knowledge and practical knowledge, consider work as a situated activity capable of generating, by working, further knowledge. Fargion (2013) argues that the reflective practitioner, in paying attention to the person and to the diversity of the situations he or she is called upon to deal with, must be able to organize and structure his or her practical action by making use of theoretical and systematic reflection on the intervention itself. In this sense, reflexive social workers implement reasoned processes that alternate through trial and error, which have nothing standardized, but which allow them to acquire the awareness that, in the implementation of an intervention, ongoing reflection can highlight the positive or negative effects of their action in order to produce innovative change (Sicora, 2005). In this sense, as Riva (2009) states, professionalism and training constitute the essential elements for the growth, development and dissemination of knowledge. Putting practices at the center means studying the experiences of those involved and building knowledge from the so-called practical wisdom, in this case of social workers and the expertise gained from those who experience problems directly. What has been said so far has contributed to the consolidation of a strand of social studies called Practice Research (i.e., practical knowledge studies). Inscribing reflective practice in the logic of research, adopting a rigorous and systematic way of proceeding, not only ensures transparency of process and intersubjective confrontation; but would allow knowledge to cross situational boundaries in a heuristic way. Practice Research, in focusing on knowledge developed through experience, and thus, the practical wisdom of practitioners, departs from Evidence Based Practice (EBP), which is the application of scientific research to the method of social service intervention. According to this current, when the social worker has to give a solution to the person, he or she will refer to the probability of successful intervention based on the user's characteristics (age, gender, type of problem). This epistemological shift unfolds in the shift from a conception of knowledge, understood as an object, to one of knowledge, understood as a practical activity, and leads to considering work practices as the locus of learning, working and innovating. At this time, as Fargion (2013) would say, social service research, in Europe as in Italy, is still in its infancy, yet there are many authors who point to the valorization of knowledge produced through research and experimentation. The social work profession may find itself caught between the enterprise of governing uncertainty or being overwhelmed by it, and the risk of becoming alternately insecure or conversely overly rigid. While uncertainty urges the need for constant research and new construction of knowledge, all forms of knowledge cannot be thought of as mechanical. The social worker treads uncertain and ambiguous ground, and in this sense is an inherently research profession, but the intertwining of research and practice requires processes of reflection and thinking (Fargion, 2021). As Schon (1983) would say, some professionals, among whom we include social workers, do not face well-defined situations. In this case, the professional's task would be to classify the problem, relate it to theoretical categories, and finally find the best pathways to resolution. Instead, it can be said that the essence of a social worker's work is to create an interaction with people who often experience a magmatic, undefined, fluctuating situation. This interaction must be built through a dialogue based on the ability to interrogate situations, ask questions and study ways to deal with them. It is a dialogue that is developed through a confrontation with different knowledge (psychologists, family members, etc.) and that leads to the production of more possible scenarios and ways to deal with the situation. The social worker cannot call himself or herself out of whatever scenario he or she constructs; in fact, he or she must be aware that the moment he or she produces an interpretation of reality he or she is already acting on it and modifying it.

2.3. Interactionism

Along the lines of the phenomenological tradition, in sociology represented by Schutz (1979), practices are to be understood as activities assimilated to unreflected and embedded habits. Such conducts have been treated insofar as they contribute to the reproduction of a working community, sometimes assuming a perpetuity of the conducts themselves which in turn contributes to the stability of the social order, recalling Bourdieu's concept of *habitus* (1990). This theoretical connection is well explained by Bartholini (2016) who states that a profession is defined as the result of a process of abstraction that concerns on the one hand the contents (i.e., knowledge and skills), and on the other hand the enucleation of the distinguishing features, skills, of the profession of the social worker. This is done on the basis of a habitus that is the result of sharing a social space that allows all members of that professional community to have the same perception of the practices put in place. The habitus, considered in this sense as a "structured structure" possesses a bond of dependence on the social world (Bourdieu, 1979) that is not modifiable and that organizes not only practices but also the perception of practices. And it is precisely in the definition of the professional skills that typify the profession of the social worker that, for example, the gap between recognized characteristics (e.g., scientific and management skills) and lower-level characteristics (e.g., interpersonal skills) is implemented. It is hypothesized, however, that the concept of practice does not imply a denial of testing and questioning skills. But what do social workers actually do when they work? And how do they spend their daily lives in the workplace? Defining social workers' work as situated activity, taking up phenomenology, ethnomethodology and symbolic interactionism, means analyzing work practices as modes of action and knowledge emerging in situ from the dynamics of interactions. Goffman (1959), making use of theatrical terminology examines the social interactions that take place in everyday life. The actor plays a script, wearing certain clothes to interpret and assume within the social context a specific role. In the Goffmian view, role is intertwined with the concept of "Self"; this is dynamic, changing. The self is nothing but a dramaturgical artifice; a product of social interactions. According to the author's thinking, social interactions refer back to the concept of framing. The frame is nothing but an interpretive framework that enables the subject to understand everyday experiences and give them meaning; it is essential for actors to take part in the scene for the recognition of their role. In addition, it is important to emphasize that the subject's aptitude for adapting to a specific interpretive scheme, and filling a specific role, is not innate but rather assimilated through experience. It is the application of the primary framework, i.e., the system of beliefs, rules that the subject learns in the course of daily experience that enables the individual to adapt to reality; in fact, the absence of this step implies the impracticality of the framing process since the initial action to be enacted in order to interpret a situation and, consequently, to be able to orient oneself knowledgeably within it is made possible by the primary frameworks. However, from the moment the subject exerts a selective influence on reality, it can take on different characteristics since it is a social construction that changes in relation to the one who encodes it, that is, with respect to the way it is interpreted. So since the participants of the interaction themselves exert an influence on the interpretive schemes to know, to understand the roles embodied by the subjects within the social interaction, we can assume that situated activity, therefore, is a frame within which it is not the context that dictates the subject to embody certain roles, on the contrary, the latter are the result of a voluntary interpretation of reality by the subjects themselves. An interpretation based in turn by the fact that situated activity is a primary framework. Continuing with a micro perspective, reference must be made to the theory of Hughes (1958), who intended to analyze work as a social interaction. His interactionist approach spread from the 1950s, and analyzed occupations as practices of everyday life, distancing itself from functionalism and the very image that the occupations themselves postulated (Hughes, 1958; Becker, 1962). According to Hughes, interactions among people result in, "different tasks and different outcomes that are part of a whole, to the production of which all in some measure contribute." Starting from this perspective, interaction between people, in a situated space/time, makes work a collective and common outcome. Therefore, it is possible to sociologically define work, including that of social workers, as a situated activity, focusing the analysis on work practice as a mode of action and knowledge emerging directly from the interactions that take place. Precisely because the work of the social worker is called to respond to the varied social needs of caring for people, the relevance of the interactionist aspect cannot be overlooked. In fact, social workers play a key role in the social interaction processes that take place, within the social context, between people, institutions/Third Sector and other professionals. In order to follow up on a theoretical analysis, it is therefore necessary to understand the social complexity and interactional processes that influence the work of social workers, using the microsociological perspective. Studying work in its daily interactions means taking as a unit of analysis the work practices and their day-to-day reproductions, shifting the focus from the analysis of work as a productive moment, to work as a reproductive moment of social relations. The production of social life becomes a skilled performance (Giddens, 1994), a skilled accomplishment, as social practices are constructed, following ethnomethodology, as procedures, methods, or techniques that social actors appropriately enact. The work of the social worker can then be seen as a performance that constantly needs fine-tuning (Garfinkel, 1967).

Chapter 3
The daily work of the social worker

The daily work of the social worker is much more than performing an activity aimed at achieving a predetermined goal. Let us try to immerse ourselves in the working day of a social worker who is in charge of a facility (CAS_SPRAR) in order to show the plurality of elements involved.

Short story
Anna waits sitting in front of the PC for the notice of appointment taking with the Internal Revenue Service to arrive. It is 7 o'clock in the morning. Anna knows that to keep the site from clogging up she has to do it very early in the morning and also quickly. In the meantime she thinks about the fact that if she fails to get the appointment she will not be able to apply for the correction of XXX's tax code information, and this will result in him losing benefits. He finally manages to get the appointment, but at the Messina office because there is no one on Barcelona Pozzo di Gotto who can solve this problem. How will she get the documents to XXX in time? All she has to do is get in her car and drive 50 km to get in front of that counter. She calls Floriana and tells her that she will not be able to go to the center, there are some important things to take care of and she will have to take care of them. He also asks Floriana to send her XXX's identification papers, they might be needed. She has to put the navigator on because she actually doesn't even know where exactly to go. It is raining outside, and it is really a bad day, dark and gloomy. She decides to cut the route and exit at the first exit of the ring road, an alternative route she used to use when she went to college. After managing, with difficulty, to find a parking space, she obviously still has to wait when she arrives. She is hungry because she did not even eat breakfast due to her haste. When it comes her turn to talk to the clerk he tells her that there is an error in the tax code due to the fact that during the first entry XXX's name was not transcribed correctly. Anna knows that she cannot rail at the clerk and that he is the only one who can solve or complicate things at that moment. But she would like to scream. The two identities are not the same, but the clerk can change it and get the social security number, and more days will pass to do this. But maybe it will come in time. Returning to Barcelona PG, trying to get to the center as quickly as possible, Anna thinks that maybe it is not a bad thing that her contract ends in

a few months. (Anna, AS CAS-SPRAR Center Director, 37 years old- 10 years of work experience)

The piece shows how to achieve a simple goal (obtaining a tax code) requires complex skills, and involves the whole person. First, Anna is involved with the body: traveling from her home 30 miles away, which requires her to take the car, park, wait in line. The five senses are all at work, and the body mediates different perceptions that contribute to diminishing the sense of pleasantness given by the performance of the activity. Anna's communication and interpersonal skills are also part of this same body, so she knows that she cannot rail against the clerk, partly because she may need him again tomorrow, so this is an interaction mode that is undergirded by her work. Second, it could be argued that Anna is also at work with her mind, because of the cognitive work required to reach the indicated office: where exactly is the place where she needs to go? What path to take to get there? From the way Anna unravels these questions we can see that this cognitive work does not follow an abstract logic, but refers to situated knowledge. It is not by chance that Anna puts on the navigator but decides which road to take, resorting to her personal knowledge and experience of the road system. In this sense, it can be said that the knowledge Anna draws on is not "other" than what she derives from her daily experience, which, indeed, should be activated, since therein lies the practical solution to her question. However, it would be hasty to conclude that the success of Anna's work depends solely on her personal skills and is entirely her own individual work: she is in fact in contact with her team of practitioners (Floriana) who will replace her in the office in the morning, and provide her with the documents she needs. Thus we get a sense of how her work also depends on (and is reflected on) that of others and, more generally, requires the coordination and articulation of multiple activities, taking place in different times and spaces. Moreover, Anna's world is populated not only by human actors, but also by technologies and objects. The phone that allows her to contact Floriana. The pc where the appointment request entry platform is. The car to travel to Messina. The navigator to get to her destination. The documents that allow her to check and verify well XXX's identity. Anna's work is thus mediated by a set of elements: the body, language, prior knowledge, human and non-human actors that daily activity leads to encounter. Not only that, it is also mediated by tacit rules of the professional community of which one is a member (which is why Floriana is expected to replace her as second and subordinate to Anna), as well as to the historical, institutional and cultural context in which the work takes shape. We can conclude that while working, activities of a different nature take place. Society is produced and reproduced in its forms of labor relations, and an individual and collective professional identity is affirmed.

3.1. Working between relationship and articulation

It is possible to add that there is necessary work in order to work. In fact, working involves many other activities. The totality of these activities can be defined as "relation work" (Gherardi, 1990), the purpose of which is the maintenance and reproduction of everyday society, both in the workplace and outside it, with other social relations. The category of the relationship has been of growing interest in the study of work practices, and especially, with regard to social services a notable contribution was made in the 1980s by Donati (1983), who first presented it as a theoretical principle stating, "at the beginning there is the relationship." According to Donati, three modes of structural coupling between theoretical knowledge of reality and social practice can be hypothesized. Each mode, (traditional, constructivist, relational) relates a certain definition of social reality, with the intervention programs that allow working with the reality itself. Folgheraiter (2001) attempted to apply Pierpaolo Donati's relational sociology to social work. The social worker should work to restore to that "social that is in place" a certain degree of relationality, which is the core of that emancipatory practice that the social worker enacts (Folgheraiter, 2001). Only by doing so will social workers be able to act as catalysts of social ties and relationships that work and that are capable of producing relational positivity within the coping process, which will soon lead to the solution of a given common problem (Folgheraiter, 2009). Within a work practice, situated in time and space, relationships are woven and stabilized. But it should be kept in mind that working and spending part of the day engaged in work activities is only one aspect of life, which in turn is made up of other activities usually intertwined with everyday life. Hence, within a work practice, situated in time and space, relationships are woven and stabilized, which have emotional implications, which may go beyond the work environment.

Short story

In the reception center we basically live with them. As soon as we arrive, they are there, because they are also very affectionate, maybe we have a chat, then we provide shifts for cleaning, check things done, they express problems to us, or they want to be supported and helped to do something, homework for example. A lot of times they are even urged or, in quotes, yelled at because they stay in the room all day sleeping and listening to music. The other day when I arrived I had to read the handover made by the educator who had done the night and reported a fight between three of them over something trivial: the use of the bathroom. She had actually called me at night but I have learned to keep my cell phone off. I have two phone cards. One I use for work and the other for family and friends. That way I can shut off when I get home. I had previous experiences that engulfed me and now I am more careful about my personal life. (Marta, Welcome Center, 41 years old- 13 years work experience).

The first element of risk, which can take on the relational dimension, and from which we start is that of the everyday life that social workers are called upon to experience in carrying out their work within refugee/asylum seeker reception centers. Through the narrative above, it is possible to identify some of the elements that give meaning to their work practice. The residential nature of the centers requires that for a long time a physical and emotional space is shared between social workers and migrants. The community is the place where both are called to live together, and where the centrality of the relationship emerges clearly. In this relationship that is nurtured day by day, every gesture and every word becomes part of the work practice. This circumstance leads social workers to intervene directly in the daily dimension of migrants, and experience a profession that sometimes requires immediate, urgent, indispensable interventions. But a key point of focus is "storytelling among female colleagues," which enables them to pool everything and interpret daily events that some may have witnessed. The social worker can thus cope with difficulties and have shared tools useful for understanding routines. But the work that social workers do, like all work based on the relationship with the other, involves the need to mediate between emotional load accumulated in the work activity and the dimension of private life. This is a significant problem that is responded to in different ways depending on the relationship to professionalism. Some implement a clear separation between the public/work dimension and the private dimension, the need not to confuse the plane of service with the plane of feelings and friendship: professionalism is service delivery, not relationship delivery. This idea of clear separation, expressed by the interviewee, not con-founding between work and private life, appears as a defense that allows them to safeguard the construction of their own family and emotional sphere. Being totally available is not in itself considered as a source of balance between the different moments of one's living. And when one fails to give a boundary, which can also be the temporal boundary that materializes in the always-accessible cell phone, the risk is that the person is shipwrecked. This can lead to the risk of losing personal spaces. One can generate a difficulty in holding the emotional impact with the work and identifying with it. All this leads back to the theme of bornout, which concerns all those professions that can be defined as higt-touch, that is, in continuous and direct contact with people in difficulty. Ferrario (2004) speaks of it in terms of "elastic professionalism," in that it is always at risk of "breaking down," due to an extreme adaptability on the part of the social worker who assumes an anarchic mode, which leads them to accept all kinds of requests and solicitations, thus preventing the application of any other norms and any definition and delimitation of work time and space. The questions that this perspective raises are particularly important for reflection on the plane of training and professionalism, especially with respect to the nexus between service and relationality, between professionalism and friendship. For some social workers, this nexus is configured in terms of conflict, or at least with a need to "detach" from the emotional baggage accumulated on the job, with different modalities and motivations that nevertheless have in common the need to protect their family relationships. For others, on the other hand, this relationship arises in terms of harmony: the possibility of feeling fulfilled, giving one's best at work, becomes an element of balance with respect to oneself and family relationships. Therefore, what allows a balance in the concrete relationship with one's work is not the caesura, but the acquisition of an awareness, of a reflective capacity in relation to the emotions and the intensity of the relationships crossed. This is an awareness that is built over time and that can help the social worker to question the elements of omnipotence that often characterize the beginnings of the profession, and which has led to review, through the accumulation of experience, the contradictory and complex aspects of the relationship. Only through mindfulness work and reflexivity will it be possible to gather all the richness of relationships, reckoning with and accepting the fact that this capacity for openness has emotional costs, has a burden. Between these two types of positions, the one reported by the interviewee and the one we advocate, lie multiple other possibilities. For reasons of brevity we will not include interview excerpts that narrate these positions, but there was no shortage of interviewees' accounts of fears and burdens. These are also some of the imprints that this kind of work leaves within life experiences: fears that creep into the private, and question the interviewees not only as professionals but as parents, children, etc. The theme that seems to tie all these interviews together is the desire not to be overwhelmed by the suffering of the relationship. One tries to respond with forms of defense that allow one to continue to cope with the day-to-day work. Rather than a theme, we could speak of a complex and articulated condition that affects the work practice of social workers and others, and which we will go into more detail in the last section of Chapter 5, when we discuss illness narrative.

But it should be kept in mind that working and spending part of the day engaged in work activities is only one aspect of life, which in turn is made up of other activities usually intertwined with everyday life. Relationship work is not the only work that is done alongside work as a direct transformative activity. Alongside it we can see that a great deal of work is done in order to make sure that the work activity can be carried out smoothly. This is what Corbin and Strauss (1993) refer to as articulation work, that is, the work of establishing, maintaining and changing the arrangements necessary to work both within one's own organizational unit and between different units. In the case of social workers dealing with the reception of refugees/asylum seekers, much of the articulation work takes place in the interaction with both external professionals (belonging to municipalities, the Prefecture, the ASL, the Internal Revenue Service, etc.) and other internal professionals (psychologists, educators, pedagogists, etc.). The social worker who directs a reception center needs to make arrangements with the Prefecture and the municipality in order to do his or her job, and without these arrangements he or she would have no way of being sure that places are available, that job placements or work grants are scheduled, that visits are conducted, etc. The set of these interactions are routinely established within and between units through a series of collaborative and competitive strategies that require negotiation and persuasion. But that once established do not last forever; indeed, they often break down (or break down) because of unforeseen events, employee changes, and contingencies that require further articulation work. For example, when unforeseen events happen, work is delayed, loses quality, or simply cannot be completed. And this generates conflicts, anxieties, frustrations, and further work to repair the social relationship that has been broken and must recreate itself. Simple, everyday ruptures of normalcy thus require work to repair and renegotiate previous arrangements.

> Short story
> *During one day in Covid-19 period, two workers became ill and could not attend work. It came difficult for me director (social worker) to replace them. I did not have the power to request and hire more staff on the spur of the moment, and the only thing I could do was to personally engage and ask her colleagues to change shifts. Unfortunately, one of the educators was out with a small group of boys who had been taken to a friendly game with the school team. I had tried to re-frame everyone's shifts and ensure coverage within the facility, but the educator and the small group of boys returned later because the game (with final greetings and awards) lasted longer than expected. When the fellow educator arrived, he tried to explain that the delay was not caused by him, and in the end the colleagues who had remained in the facility, already filling in, had to extend their shifts further. I had to investigate to identify the causes of the delay, trying to make peace between the educator and other colleagues. (Isabella, AS Minors Center, 30 years- 3 years work experience)*

This example regarding articulation work shows us how the execution of work is a collective and coordinated action. It is not enough that the division into the different shifts and its different specificities has, at one time, been made. It must be continually re-made, that is, reproduced on a daily basis. Since even within the Centers there are so many different kinds of work and tasks, agreements are needed on what is to be done, at what times, with what objectives, in what places, with what resources, and so on. All of this constitutes the work of articulation. But agreements must be reached, kept in place, and revised, through a process of continuous arrangement that includes a variety of interaction strategies such as negotiation, discussion, training, persuasion, threat, or coercion. Corbin and Strauss (1993) analyze articulation work based on three points:

1. the agreements (or arrangements) that are made between people within the same business unit, or between different units. These are arrangements that have as their object the actions necessary for the work to be carried out. For example, within a reception center there is an agreement on what work is to be carried out, who is to do it, with what resources, for how long, for what purpose. Or with different units, such as between the Prefecture and the Reception Center there is agreement with respect to resources, available places, execution time, space, expertise. What needs to

be emphasized is that agreements can exist between organizations and also between institutions, and they are always temporary and subject to renegotiation. For this very reason, articulation work can be considered a day-to-day job.

2. Settling things, i.e., the interaction strategies through which agreements are established, kept in place, and revised. These are interaction strategies in response to what is said and done by others before the work begins, and at the stage when agreements are established. Possible strategies consist of negotiating, making compromises, arguing, educating and persuading, dominating and controlling, and so on.
3. attitude (or stance), that is, the position each participant takes toward both the work and the processes of "working things out." These are the positions each person takes in relation to how he or she perceives his or her power to control and influence the situation and context in which arrangements are made. Individual attitudes also depend on, and change in response to, the attitudes of others.

The concept of articulation work therefore encompasses all the activities necessary in a workplace to perform the work itself. But we must also consider some particular nuances. When, for example, we talk about service work, it is important to consider and emphasize the importance of arbitrage (Grosjean and Lacoste, 1999), that is, when agreement needs to be reached on values, orders of magnitude, and understanding of the appropriate action of the situation. In short, cases in which the deontological dimension of the profession is called into question. And this is what often happens for social workers. The collective production of rules of behavior, based on values, constitutes a dimension of work that cannot be underestimated since it is social groups that produce, legitimize, observe and respect rules while working and dealing with practical problems.

Another concept that may be in line with the previous ones is the one developed by Engestrom (2008), the "knotworking," and which recalls the idea of networking as weaving relationships. This expression suggests that it is not enough just to weave relationships, but that they must be fixed, knotted and made relatively solid and constant, including by means of ad hoc objects or practices. The network of relationships is in fact knotworking, nodes and ties in a system that tighten or loosen according to the object on which effort converges at varying degrees of intensity.

There may be times of increased intensity of interaction, given the need of the situation, and then loosening and only weak ties exist. Weak ties are understood to mean that a connection persists over time between those involved but is not active. Only at specific moments do the ties reactivate, the nodes tighten, and the network becomes productive again. Tying the knot becomes a self-organizing activity that relies on the practical knowledge of those who identify and solve a problem. This, for example, is what happens when all the actors, involved in various capacities in reception, get together to discuss around a table with respect to what to do. What is therefore done when working is much more complex and articulated than simply performing a scheduled activity. And the social worker's work context cannot be considered only as container of work activity. The work activity can be studied as an expertice that, in addition to following a script, must have a situated interpretation. Granovetter (1973) also helps us think about networks by arguing that weak ties are particularly useful in providing new job opportunities because they introduce new labor market information into a larger social network. The author states that people are socially disadvantaged if they do not have networks of weak ties and connect to their own strong network of ties of close friends and family members. People are more likely to learn about new job opportunities through acquaintances (weak ties) than through close friends (strong ties), because acquaintances are more likely to be aware of information that is not known to them and their close friends. Consequently, a knowledge network, or weak ties, will be a low-density network in which many of the potential relationships have yet to be established. Weak ties theory was developed in relation to job search, but in the broader social network theory it also describes the spread of disease, the proliferation of ideas and the evolution of species, so it is ubiquitous in every structure and service system. Put another way, take for example a person, A, who has a very strong network of close friends, most of whom know each other as well as A. At the same time, B has an equivalent strong network of close, close friends. Within these two networks there is a lot of duplication and very little newness. What A knows and shares with a few friends spreads rapidly through his network because everyone knows everyone. Information spreads exponentially because what A tells three people is told by them to three people each, and from there to three more people. Because most of these people are connected, the information quickly becomes redundant in the sense that everyone has already heard it. The same is true for B's network. But when A and

B come together, they not only create the value of sharing what each of them knows individually, whether knowledge, skills or access, but they also create a bridge between their two much larger but closed networks. A and B are weak ties; acquaintances with very little duplication between their networks and knowledge (Granovetter, 2012) and have the potential to bring new ideas, information and people into their own network. In this way they have value for others and by connecting these two networks they create value (Borgattiand Halgin, 2011). Granovetter (2012) concludes from this that his argument about the importance of weak ties does not mean that all weak ties are valuable, only those that serve as bridges between networks of strong ties have special value. It is possible that many weak ties do not become bridges, and therefore have no value in this context, however, he argues that strong ties are unlikely to create bridges, and most bridges will be weak ties.

3.2. Situated activity to practical knowledge

In the 1990s, the concept of situated action was introduced in the field of artificial intelligence and the study of human-computer interaction, as opposed to the abstract representation model of knowledge. Its most significant representatives are Winograd and Flores (1986) and Suchman (1987). These scholars use this expression to argue that in order to design good interfaces it is better to study people's concrete use of computers, rather than focusing on how people think or what they do with computers. These authors are also joined by Lave (1988) whose socio-pedagogical studies contribute to the debate by showing how abstract knowledge is not transferable to the real world, and how between knowing in everyday situations and decontextualized knowledge there is a substantial difference. The concept of situated action is then reworked by Conein and Jacopin (1994) who reconstruct its intellectual roots and relate it to later developments. It is possible to place the concept of situated action alongside the thought of Schutz (1979) and Mead (1934), that is, taking up the interactionist approach. The latter two authors started from the assumption that as all work activities presuppose an ego-referenced space composed of objects, situated action is also anchored in space. Indeed, they emphasized that the experience of contact with the objects of manipulation constituted the support for the performance of work. Schutz identifies work as a world "within reach," that is, an activity that simultaneously depends on and constitutes context. Mead, on the other hand, makes a distinction between the object in the region of manipulation, which can be seen and touched, and the object at a distance, out of reach but present in the field of visual perspective. The author thus comes to show how the work space is progressively constituted in the course of manipulative activity with tools and objects. Tools mediate activities because they enable us to do things we could not otherwise do. Technology is increasingly in extension of our bodily capabilities and increasingly incorporates knowledge and intelligence. The manipulative activity presupposes a reciprocal construction of space and action, since the action of putting objects at hand demarcates the boundaries of the same space that is being constructed. In this sense, the workplace is an active context, and not just a container of activity. It helps us remember and allows us to do some things and not do others. It prompts us to report our action and interrogates us with programs that help us suggest interventions or otherwise. The current of the situated action approach extends the original idea of work as interaction to include action with objects in relation to the physical environment and situations. The interest of this current, and the research methodology it develops, is aimed at understanding how work environments, equipped with artifacts and objects, can play a guiding role in facilitating task performance for those who work in them. What we can understand through the situated action paradigm is that the context is not a true container but a resource for action. And also, another important thing, is that the expression situated action traditionally has a privileged relationship with the idea of the "Other" and Goffman's (1956) elaboration linking it to communication. In fact, the author developed a situational theory using the expression "situated activity system" or encounter. When two people communicate, they mutually make manifest and thus accessible a space of attention, and their action is situated because it is oriented and dependent on the action of the receiver of the communication. Situation is the result of the interaction between the two people. Referring to what happens when two people communicate, making mutually manifest, and thus accessible, a space of attention. So defining an action as situated means thinking of the organization of action as emerging in situ from the dynamics of interactions. This can be composed of two processes: (a) each participant's understanding of the action of the other(s); (b) the perceived interpretation of indicators coming from the surrounding environment. Central to the situated action paradigm is the revisiting of the concept of context, which cannot be considered as a container for action, but as a situation in which the interests of the actors and the opportunities of the environment meet and mutually define each other. Thus, in work, interactions with others, situated communication, the construction of the situation, and the relationship with the physical environment and objects assume centrality, but above all the idea that these elements are held together and express a contextual logic to the situation. For example, in the social worker's work, the interview phase with the person helps us better understand this:

> Short story
>
> *Every time I have to do an interview I try to prepare myself not only in terms of information but also in terms of space. For example, the desk I move it so many times, because the front position is not always what is needed. And then I often have to lock in the drawer all the stacks of folders that are on it. Also the pc, if I don't need it I prefer to keep it off during an interview. Having it on might distract me or the person. Not to mention the pictures that are on both the desk and the desk. I usually remove all these items because they can be objects that get between me and communication with the person. (Barbara, AS Common, 54 years old- 27 years work experience)*

In the case of the social worker and the person, their action is situated because it is oriented and dependent on the action of the recipient of the communication. In short, the situation is the result of interaction. In this sense, studying work as practical knowledge and situated activity can be said to be constituted with the intention of replacing objective rationality (decontextualized rationality) with the logic of the situation (contextual rationality). For example, as we have seen from the interview above, the context in which social workers perform their work is not pre-constituted; rather, it is actively constructed in many situational frameworks that interpret situations by cutting them out of the environment. The work of the social worker in this sense becomes a "savoir faire" that is, a knowing how to contribute daily the working practices of the professional community within which one works and cooperates. Starting precisely from the perspective of work as situated action, it is then possible to arrive at the perspective of work as practical knowledge.

3.3. Work practices

The situated action paradigm, which we have previously introduced, prompts us to study knowledge that is encapsulated in practice. In this sense, knowledge is qualified as practice, as an activity, rather than as a body of knowledge. And thus it too can be analyzed as a situated activity, that is, emerging from the context of its production and anchored by the material supports of its production environment. We can say that practical knowledge is contextual knowledge that is contrasted with theoretical knowledge as decontextualized knowledge. Generally, the adjective "practical" referring to knowledge has a belittling evaluative emphasis: practical knowledge is that which is acquired by doing, which does not need to function, and is therefore a commodity of modest value. The common sense of this statement is challenged today precisely by the characterization of contemporary society as a knowledge society (Castells, 1996) or cognitive capitalism (Boutang, 2002). The more work becomes dematerialized, the more knowledge becomes one of its main products. Working in social work means using a body of knowledge as resources for action. And working generates additional knowledge. Thus, working is knowing and not simply applying acquired knowledge. Take for example the practice of online interviewing, which occurred especially in the Covid-19 period. The social worker connects via app with the person; the connection can be made from the office or from home (smart working). The service takes the form of a "remote interview," and the activity that emerges from this new mode of work, distributed in space, is substantially different from the face-to-face interview. It is neither an office interview nor a home interview. The distance interview, therefore, takes the form of a new type of social service practice, a kind of hybridization of pre-existing practices, which forces both the person and the social worker to learn new ways of communicating and working. The new distributed setting, made possible by new technologies, requires the person/social worker to learn to act in a sociomaterial system that is characterized by the different types of knowledge spread across different subjects, objects and relationships. It is therefore a matter of activating practical knowledge that involves knowledge that has been learned during university education and refined during work experience, but which is not reduced to the situational application of pre-existing knowledge.

Let's look at what can be considered a typical example:

Short story
During Covd-19, when we were doing online interviews on behalf of the counseling center where I work as a social worker, I came across the case of a Nigerian woman. She was a beautiful, very young girl who had been sexually assaulted before her arrival in Italy and now found herself pregnant. The girl had approached us through the urging of a compatriot of hers who had also

needed counseling years earlier. I managed to retrieve the file and noted that she had claimed to have had other miscarriages in the past. Once I started the online interview I quickly realized that it would be even more complicated to communicate because the girl did not speak Italian well, and she often could not understand what I was saying. She appeared very concerned and listened to me, answering my questions only with small nods of her head. I tried to ask her how she felt but her answer was simply a movement with her head. I realized that I had to find a solution, I had to get her to tell me what was going on so, since I could not have a mediator by my side, I desperately decided to look for a translator online. I asked the girl to write to me in the chat room, in her language how she felt and what she had, and from time to time I translated with the translator. Eventually I understood that as a result of some brown spotting, the girl thought she had lost the baby and wanted to know where to go for a visit. So I invited her to go to the obstetric emergency room, explaining that she would not have to wait in a long line and that through an ultrasound they would know if everything was okay. (Katia, AS Health Service, 52 years old- 23 years work experience)

We have in this case a person who is not well, and a remote interview alone is not enough to understand his or her needs. The social worker mobilizes a knowledge related to theoretical knowledge and one from translation tools (online translator) to come to a decision. But if we limit ourselves to this interpretation, we would not be able to see the work of articulating the various knowledge mobilized during these few minutes of conversation. We then need to reconstruct the network of relationships within which the practice takes place in order to be able to bring to light the nodes that anchor the different knowledges and to see how these constitute the resources that are mobilized in order to carry out the conversation at a distance. If we analyze this sociologically, from a methodological point of view, we have to ask what is the network that anchors the distributed and fragmented knowledge that shapes the distance interview. Then we are able to see how it resides:

- in the person-who possesses and brings into the long-distance interview knowledge of his or her own body and sensations. Knowledge in this case, is the ability to perceive an "abnormality" and translate it into an account through language and the narration of symptoms. This initial description and knowledge is supported by leaks, which translate the patient's subjective knowledge into scientific knowledge;
- the social worker-the social worker's expert knowledge is expressed precisely in the transformation of the person's idiomatic expressions

into "objective" knowledge, through the use of the translator and the application of expertise applied to common sense;
- in organizational rules, the intervention protocol is based on the segmentation of the intervention process into a proper sequence of micro-actions, and appear to be the result of a process of rationalization of knowledge. In carrying out the interview at a distance, the social worker, follows a protocol that allows him or her to structure the conversation with the person;
- in artifacts-knowledge resides not only in human beings and rules, but also in artifacts, technologies and objects that participate in and constitute the setting of the activity. In the case under consideration, the person-fiche that the social worker has to fill out not only defines the sequence and content of the questions, but also represents a tool of organizational accountability (redirection). People make their actions explicable at the very moment they name and act them. Similarly to the card-person, there is also another artifact that shapes medical knowledge through the constraints and rules it places. It is the online translation software, which creates the constraints on the writing of the interview report, and that makes accontable not so much the activity or interaction with the social worker, but the rationality that in retrospect reconstructs the dialogue that took place, in terms of legal responsibility as well;
- the technological infrastructure—the online interview is made possible by a technological infrastructure, made up of computers, cables, telephones, cell phones, etc. The practical knowledge mobilized by the remote interview is thus anchored in a technological infrastructure that when it works makes the interview possible.

Knowledge, therefore, is not just in the social worker's head; it is anchored in the material world, and working involves activating a fragmented knowledge system. All social workers interacting within a specific work practice possess pieces of knowledge that, like jigsaw puzzles, must be aligned with other tiles to gain intelligibility. I have used the example of distance interviewing to show how what we call "knowledge" is a cooperative activity, a practical accomplishment, but also to focus attention on the now technologically dense environments and how new technologies enter (and have entered) the practice of the social worker, especially as a result of Covid-19. In distance interviewing, the introduction of new technologies indeed entails a dematerialization of work. Observing, as well as watching and listening to the person, are typical activities of the social worker that disappear within the remote interview, resulting in the loss of sensory skills. There is also an impoverishment of the linguistic-objective basis of knowledge, replaced by a reduction in communicative competence. The patient's language is expressed without the body, and mediated through technology (translator) so translation activity occurs only on a linguistic basis, within a rarefied interactive space.

Chapter 4
Body-mediated knowledge

4.1. Body and practical knowledge

Practical knowledge is tacit, that is, it is produced through the body and stored in it. This means that practical knowledge is mediated by the body, and that this same body constitutes a resource in order to gain professional insight and support a work performance that appears competent. From the perspective of work as a practical and situated activity, however, looking at the body means grasping its expressive potential as well as its sensory meditations. Focusing on the body allows thematizing work as a performative activity, in which coordination in space and synchrony in timing, constitute fundamental skills. To explicitly thematize the theme of the body and sensory knowledge within working, let us try starting with another account of our interviewees:

Short story
One day a report came to the municipality from some neighbors who, despite numerous attempts to meet and complaints, complained about the state of disrepair in an apartment adjoining theirs. When I called the owner to make an appointment I thought that after all, the neighbors had gone too far; from the tone of voice and her words, the situation seemed under control and nothing serious. When we arrived at the place the first thing that struck us was the continuous barking of the dog coming from that apartment. I thought from the stench coming all the way outside and the chaos of the dog that someone was lying dead in that apartment. Yet I had talked to that girl by phone. The windows were completely closed. We tried to ring but there was probably no electricity. We therefore began to knock. The girl who opened the door seemed to be waiting for us. She let us in with considerable embarrassment. The dog was almost afraid of us and as soon as we opened the door he came out, and it was difficult for the girl to bring him back in. The scene that awaited us was unbelievable. The floor could not be seen, and everything was completely filled with all kinds of garbage. Moreover, everywhere there was dog poop. On the mattress, on the couch, on the

floor. The stench made people want to throw up. All of a sudden my colleague had to go outside because she felt sick. I didn't really know how to move, I was trying to show a nonchalant attitude but in reality I felt terrible. I didn't even know where to put my feet. Several times I was in danger of losing my balance, and there was nothing to hold on to. Every object, table, chairs, furniture, were completely full of stuff to throw away and in an obvious state of decomposition. Not to mention the condition of the bathroom. Clogged with water and sewage covering the entire floor. It was creepy. Throughout the visit, all I could do was ask myself, "How can a human being live in these conditions?" (Sabrina, AS Commune, 60 years- 37 years work experience)

Interestingly, the social worker begins this imaginative-empathic observation (Strati, 2004) in an almost causal way. As she approaches the doorway, the dog's barking attracts her attention. He tries to decipher what he is hearing, and produces judgments about the danger he seems to sense. Judgments that spring, as soon as she goes inside, from her imagining herself in that girl's place, and thus have their origin in empathy rather than analytical distance. This account allows us to delineate two characteristics of sensitive knowledge:

- sensitive knowledge is the kind of knowledge that passes through our perceptual faculties (sight, hearing, smell, taste and touch). In this sense, it is knowledge that comes from the body, of a prereflexive nature, and to the body it remains in order to be stored and then transmitted;
- sensitive knowledge is not neutral, in the sense that with one's body a person feels and judges, acts and exhibits in organizational and work practice one's difference and personal knowledge (Strati, 2004).

One knows through the body therefore. The body is the first mediation with those outside of us. Sensible knowledge is learned through the five senses. It is largely tacit, but social knowledge. In many workplaces it is the senses that give the measure of achievement, just as they symbolize the competence expressed in having an eye, having an ear, having insight. The material world is a second great mediation of both doing and knowing. It lives with us, around us and through us. It is not inert matter when we say that the material world interpellates us. Through this account emerges the body and the knowledge gained through the senses: sight, hearing, touch (in the description provided by the girl) that become essential elements. The body and the senses somehow give "meanings" to what we experience. What is important for us to understand is that, however subjective, all these elements are not innate or the result of cognitive work, but are learned in the course of working and refined in the course of performing activities. Sensory knowledge is preriflexive: it precedes language and reflection on experience and is therefore guided by the whole body, rather than by the mind alone. As Strati (2004) notes, As Strati (2004) notes there is indeed difficulty from of formalizing the instructions and actions to be taken to address and prospect an intervention. And it is the same kind of difficulty a social worker might have in arguing how it is more (or less) right to intervene in a case. In the case of social workers we are dealing with work that involves the bodily element, and there is therefore this tendency to bring human experience back within bodily categories. As phenomenology (Merleau-Ponty, 1945) and sociology itself (Simmel, 1908) have already argued, we all have a body, and thus, is this at the societal level an element on which to base common experience: the body is the physical place from which people experience and know. In this sense, knowledge can interrogate other forms of knowledge. Practical knowledge thus comes through the body, sensitive knowledge and judgment. Finally, the social worker's body is also at work through sight, and above all, the acquisition of a professional gaze is probably part of any working career. Goodwin (1994) considers sight not only from a physiological perspective, but as an exquisitely social and cultural activity, oriented according to the cognitive tasks that must be performed within given professional frames. For example, the author analyzed the context of a courtroom to show the subtle work of negotiation through which vision, definitions and descriptions of some event or phenomenon are stabilized by means of interaction, words, gestures and glances. Indeed, each professional field tends to shape its own professional vision. That is, to communally construct the way of seeing the world, to identify the relevant properties of objects with respect to one's own peculiar activity. Consider, for example, the case of the home interview carried out by the social worker in this story. What the social worker has to do is to start with a detailed analysis of the process of visual education that makes the social worker learn to look, and later learn to see what is happening inside that apartment. It is obvious that an experienced social worker must know at first glance the trace of problematic elements. Education in seeing is not a private and occasional experience, but a relationship that is sustained over time within precise activities. It is followed by discursive practices, physical interaction, particular places, and objects that encode attention and incorporate professional knowledge deemed relevant within a particular scope of activity, which may be, for example, that of home interviewing. What is seen therefore is constituted and made meaningful by the way it is positioned within a larger set of practices (Goodwin, 2000), even to the point of becoming an epistemic framework useful for understanding the portion of reality that pertains to particular activities. What is important to emphasize is how in the acquisition of a professional vision the whole body learns to see, and through observation, learns to perceive and classify phenomena, as well as what are the cognitive standards deemed valid within a given work domain. It should also be remembered that bodies are gendered and such differences acquire meaning within a symbolic imaginary that is that of gender, which invites us, not here, to reflect on a further element namely that work practice (and the knowledge situated in it) is never neutral, but activates and (re)produces specific gendered choices (Di Rosa, Gui, 2021).

4.2. Tacit knowledge

In the situated action paradigm, we must consider Polany's (1958) contribution and the concept of tacit knowledge to emphasize the way in which the body embodies cognitive processes. Tacit knowledge stands for precisely those knowledges that cannot be made explicit or rationalized in words, and how these are learned through the body, imitation or forms of knowledge transmission that do not go through cognition but through interpersonal relationships. Polany (1958) brought the example of riding a bicycle and how one learns to do so. According to the author, "The theoretical knowledge of maintaining balance says that for every angle of lack of balance you curve the deflection inversely proportional to the square of the speed at which you are going" (Polany, 1958, p. 135). But it is not on the basis of this explicit knowledge that one can teach or learn to ride a bicycle. If a person did so, he or she would risk falling. There are in fact other contextual factors that must be taken into account, and which are not made explicit in the previous rule. Rules of know-how, Polany concludes, may be useful but they do not determine practice. Rather, they constitute maxims that can serve as guides, but only if they are integrated into practical knowledge. Riding a bicycle, speaking, listening, etc. are not learned through a manual or explicit rules describing how to do it. It takes practice. And this is learned with one's own body. All trades and jobs are based on

Tacit knowledge

tacit knowledge that is learned without really knowing how it is learned or that is learned explicitly. But then one forgets the steps through which one learned it. Trivially, one knows how to do it even if one does not know how to explain it in words. Sociology has provided numerous examples of the way the body and senses intervene in activities. Wanting to reconnect with the work of the social worker, we need only consider the work they do within a shelter. In these places, education of the body also comes through the habit of listening to what is said by colleagues, or other professionals. And the skill lies in automatically initiating certain actions the moment you hear certain words. So you learn to pay attention to a whole range of words. Think, for example, of governance moments, thematic tables, memoranda of understanding, etc. where social workers are summoned to participate to discuss the existing and future projections.

Short story

It happened several times that we center directors were summoned to the Prefecture to discuss together with partners and promoters the outcome of some projects. I remember once witnessing a discussion between a trade unionist who was in charge of the project on migrant labor in the areas of Eastern Sicily. The unionist was complaining about the absence of controls in the area as well as services for migrants. I knew what he was talking about even though he did not actually clearly mention it. In my head I was tying up the threads of the web of exploitation and neglect that many of the boys I knew were forced to experience, though they never complained. And he did not see them as issues that concerned only refugees/asylum seekers in that eastern belt. I was trying to catch all the proposals the unionist was throwing out and began writing them down on a pad. I was saying to myself, "The situation he is complaining about is the same situation that in some cases our refugees/asylum seekers experience when they go to work in the greenhouses in Milazzo and Barcellona Pozzo di Gotto. So why not try to take a closer look at these good practices he is proposing and reproduce them, in a small way, as an experiment, in our local area?" (Alessia, AS Welcome Center, 32 years- 7 years work experience)

What also characterizes these workplaces is the way in which a common orientation and responsibility toward the outcome of the work is maintained by all professionals present. Coordination requires a mutual orientation of those who work there. A common orientation toward the development of a plurality of situations. The order of interaction is then emerging from the communications that are heard and not heard, from a continuous state of words being said and not said, to which great care must be taken.

4.3. Bodies at work

Thematizing the work done by the body, that is, those jobs in which the body is involved within certain professional domains, allows for a different analysis of another classic category of analysis in sociology, namely that of work routines. When one looks at the workplace not as a simply given set-up, but as a situational territory actively constructed by the people who work there, thematizing the work of the body allows one to think and analyze work as if it were a performance based on an improvised choice of actions to be performed and responses to be given. Let us take the case of the social worker's work at a social secretariat as a paradigmatic example of ordinary, predetermined work. Within a social secretariat there remain a number of low-skilled tasks that do not enjoy any of the benefits brought by technology in contemporary workplaces, and indeed find themselves harnessing the social worker within the same mechanisms of control and routinization of work typical of bureaucratic work. But what might it mean to work within the social secretariat for a social worker? How to get to the bottom of what social workers actually do there? How, then, does one faithfully follow a work routine, that is, always perform the same task in the same way? This is also a matter of practice. The actions of social workers working within a secretariat are geared toward producing change in the person. Far from doing the same thing over and over again, in addition to checking and entering socio-anagraphical data, they stage an improvised choice of actions, which involve not only the management of the speaking turn during the conversation, but also that of numerous other elements the first of these is the body. In fact, the arrangement of objects in the work space and the body in relation to these placements turns out to be essential for social workers to conduct the interview. During the front office for example, the social worker usually has a monitor on and inside uses a data entry platform, a kind of questionnaire/chart that she refers to. Because this is one of the things that is used to guide and understand what benefits can be granted and disbursed. Then, next to the keyboard there will also be some paper and pens, so the social worker can keep note of some useful details (not to be noted in the card on the pc) and keep the conversation going. There may also be a list with all the ISEE (income indicator) thresholds for benefits. Anyone who works in front of a desk is used to arranging items in such a way that they are within easy reach. But what is surprising is not so much the spatial organization of the work desk, but the fact that the body itself and its position becomes an integral part of the organization of the space. For example, one of the social workers interviewed had learned to enter data into the questionnaire/fiche on the PC with his left hand, and use the pen with his right hand to take notes on a separate sheet of paper. In fact, writing in pen was essential for social workers to manage the loss of information. Generated by the inflexibility of the software for example in some cases the questionnaires/schedules to be filled out do not offer the space where to insert some items, and so the social worker had to jot it down on a piece of paper because she knows that these notes could constitute important information, in order also to better analyze the need. The anticipation of events constitutes an element of the choice of action. Here, the practical knowledge of social workers becomes an essential resource that allows them to understand what the response/benefit should be for the person. More generally, it is on the basis of this practical knowledge that social workers are able to coordinate different courses of action with multiple objects (reading from paper, looking at the person, listening, typing on the pc, etc.). In short, we can say that the work of the social worker within a social secretariat resembles a performance with a choice of action: the performance is entrusted to the body of the operator, while the choice of action occurs from the different information that the operator acquires. It may seem a contradictory metaphor in that improvisation refers to an extemporaneous action from certain contingencies. But the image serves to emphasize precisely the co-presence of two components: that is, about how routine conversations are maintained from an improvised use of the elements and information at hand. So moving from the category of work routines to that of performance allows us to grasp how routines constitute, in each case, local outcomes. As Schegloff (1986) would say, this should prompt sociologists to question about the range of contingencies that can manifest themselves at different times in the activity, and how a sense of routine is reproduced. In essence, it is intended to show how, even in jobs that tend to be repetitive and bureaucratic, the routine aspects of work are neither given nor automatically manifested. Rather, they are a practical realization brought into being and reproduced by flesh-and-blood people, through a performance that involves language skills, the use of objects and technologies, and the bodies of those involved.

In conclusion, practical knowledge is anchored in the body as a cognitive resource of the event of mediating and preserving knowledge. This means that in performing a work activity, the body is a source of knowledge, makes some knowledge its own, and knows how to do more than the subject would know how to explain in purely verbal or procedural terms. Sensible knowledge (that which passes through the perceptual faculties) causes knowledge to be incorporated, to become tacit and to be, in a sense, somatized. As in the case of the social worker during the interview at the social secretariat, it was seen how the body and senses give stability, help coordinate with others, and can provide the right solution to ambiguous situations. That is, they lead to making judgments about the work being done and how it is being done. In terms of situated action, it is our interest to emphasize especially this last step, namely, the fact that the body constitutes the first mediation of the relationship with the world. One learns to see, hear, smell, etc. So the body knows. And sensitive knowledge flows within a professional vision. It becomes a characteristic of the social worker's work and the professional field of reference. Based on these considerations, therefore, it is possible to read the work of the social worker as an expressive activity more like a performance than a routine of predetermined actions. Indeed, close observation of work, such as that of the social worker, whose body is formally visible behind a desk, has made it possible to highlight how even a simple desk and conversation can constitute the situational territory that provides the resources for action. The moment one extends the analysis of the conversations carried out between social workers and people to the totality of the elements they involve, one understands how the conversation routine is the result of work involving the whole body and not just linguistic abilities. It is therefore from a body that knows how to move in space, after analysis of the elements, actions, conversation after conversation that may be relevant to performance, that the social worker makes a choice of action.

Chapter 5
The discursive practice of the social worker

So we can say, as stated so far, that social workers work with their hands, with their arms, with their heads, with their whole bodies. But they also and especially work with speech, with language, with communication that is situated in interactions. The work practice of social workers is mediated by language, whether in the form of technical vocabularies and classification systems or language in use. When we say that speaking is working, we mean that discursive practices are a tool of communication and interaction, but also something else. Extremely, we could say that the more manual work is reduced quantitatively, becomes immaterial, the more important the social worker's communicative competence is in order to work correctly and prevent misunderstandings and errors. The expansion of social services in our contemporary society, and also of interventions, makes communicative competence central, as speaking constitutes not only a communication tool, but is one of the main ingredients of social service itself. Therefore, in this chapter we will analyze the work of the social worker as a discursive practice, that is, as a doing, a knowing how to do with words.

5.1. Communicative competence

In work situations, speaking is almost never an end in itself, as Boutet and Gardin (2001) write. Speech is always tending toward a happiness, toward an action to be performed, a solution to be found, a damage to be repaired, an answer to be given. In short, toward an action or a diagram to be understood. Tracing the boundaries and internal entanglements of discourse analysis is beyond the scope of our topic, but following the thinking of Boutet and Maingueneau (2005), we can say that since the 1990s there has been a generalized increase in attention to the uses of language in specific contexts and for particular purposes. We cannot dwell here on the use of language as a specific form of activity, but we should point out that in addition to anthropology and sociolinguistics, currents of conversation analysis from the sociology of communication also contribute to discourse analysis. We are interested in language as a situated form of linguistic mediation of the social worker's work activity. We will refer to this as discursive practices. In almost all jobs, and also in that of the social worker, speaking is not only a means of working, but an actual job. Let us therefore go on to analyze in detail how communicative competence is realized in the work practice of the social worker. Communicative competence refers to the knowledge that is required to use language appropriately, for example, in relation to specific cultural contexts, such as what happens in the case of migrants seeking asylum/refugees. The social worker's work is based on "institutional conversation" for the purpose of distinguishing speaking as work from ordinary conversation. Institutional conversation is aimed at the performance of work and the reproduction of patterns of interaction that give stability to work practice. Institutional conversations effect transformation by means of speech. Practical knowledge is therefore also made up of communicative competence, that is, of knowing how to use language appropriately in relation to specific contexts of interaction. An important book for the analysis of discursive practices in institutional contexts is that of Drew and Heritage (1992) who, in analyzing different work contexts, illustrate how through situated discursive practices, certain types of work are produced in the interaction between a professional, institutional representative and the people who access institutions. By doing so in the professional-people interaction, the institution is reproduced. Consider here what Fargion (2013) explained, namely, that in many cases the institution being reproduced shows elements of conflict, such as a centralization of power, which may hinder social worker-people communication. The motivations that may lead a person to visit the social worker can be diverse (ranging from spontaneous access, to induced, intermediated, and finally to coerced access), so being able to realize the vulnerability that people bring with them because of their problems can serve the social worker to address the discursive situation. It is then the social worker's duty to have competence in asking questions to explore the person's state. Therefore, possessing language competence means, in terms of discretion implementing word choice and turn management. Indeed, some people may perceive questions as hostile or personally averse to answering them. In either case, it is an art about knowing how to ask the questions, evaluate the answers received and create a climate that neutralizes, instrumentally, the power asymmetry between the participants in that type of conversation. Also avoiding taking an overt judgment with respect to the answers. In the case, for example, of the social worker who has to dialogue with refugee/asylum-seeking migrants, the activity of giving responses must also be considered, and as Gumperz (1989) would say, to do this properly one must focus on the multicultural context. A foreigner's responses can themselves be problematic to interpret. In the interaction between social worker and refugee/asylum-seeker, one must also consider tone, speed, gestures, social context of reference and origin, etc. These examples show how the institutional contexts in which conversations between social worker and people take place represent the essence of the work, and suggest other work moments in which the management of the relationship with the person is central for the production of a service and for the management of the interpersonal relationship. There are three characteristics of institutional conversations according to Drew and Heritage (1992):

- institutional interaction involves the orientation of at least one of the participants to a purpose, task or identity specifically associated with the institutions in question. We can say that it is an instrumental discursive practice in that it is directed toward a specific purpose and usually carried out conventionally with a communicative style marked by the conventions of that specific community of professional practice;
- institutional interaction may involve the presence of specific constraints on one or both participants, who may use them as specific resources in ongoing interactions;
- institutional conversation may be associated with interpretive patterns and procedures that are specific to that particular institutional context.

Then there are differences in institutional conversations related to the type of context. For example, the phone call that a woman victim of violence makes to a social worker: this request for help will therefore be immediately oriented that way, and the conversation will typically have a top-down, i.e., top-down, pattern. Conversely, the service access that a mother with economic problems makes to the social worker generally constitutes a poorly defined task, and the institutional interaction will be more characterized by ongoing negotiation. We can define the content of this service access that will have a bottom-up, bottom-up structure. Let us look in detail at a discursive practice that can be called "giving bad news." This can also occur frequently in the social work profession, for example, let us think of the case of a child being removed from the family unit as a result of physical violence.

> Short story
>
> *I remember as if it happened yesterday a case that affected me deeply, both personally and professionally. I remember the words of this woman who said to me, "You know, my partner was acting strangely, and already there I began to have some concerns, which I sensed already in the house. And then when she came in and called me aside I immediately thought, "Oh no, I wonder what she found out!" Then she asked me, "What do you think about all this? As a mother what did you perceive?" and at that moment, seeing me crying, she told me that the child had suffered obvious violence. I in looking at her said, "It can't be!" I had never experienced abuse or violence from my partner, but suddenly I connected the crying, the drawings made at school, the peeing in the bed when my partner came home. All these things jumped out at me. And she couldn't say a word. He told me was that these are things you social workers see a lot, but they should never happen, to any child, and no mother should have these horrible thoughts and fears. There I understood that I had to take charge of my life and save my son and me as well."*
> (John, AS USSM, 58 years old- 31 years work experience).

In this situation, the clues that the social worker gives come from trying to create a kind of normalcy, and even greater intimacy and protection in the interaction with the mother. Based on the social worker's previous fears and on having noticed something strange despite never having feared it, the mother realizes that that visit will result in the removal of the child. This brief exchange of words between the social worker and the mother, shows how the one who brings bad news has difficulty presenting it in a straightforward manner, and in avoiding uttering them and merely confirming the inference of the one on the receiving end she manages to handle the transmission of the news as a collaborative activity, a co-production of the situation This is called co-impllication of the parties in the production of bad news. This device of "staging the point of view" consists of three moves:

- the social worker asks the person, in this case the mother, a question and invites her to state her opinion of the situation;
- the mother, then the recipient, responds and states her assessment;
- the social worker reports and evaluates.

Similar to the previous moves to give clues, guess and confirm, the social worker in some cases also "sets the stage" as a common feature of institutional interaction. The participants in the activity (mother and social worker in this case) are implicated in it. In this type of interaction, the social worker is able to do her job, that is, to formulate and have the intervention accepted by means of the conversation and the whole interaction that incorporates the person's point of view.

Short story

Social worker: So, how's your partner?

Mother: Good, pretty good…I talked to my partner and told him that we can't see each other anymore. And that he should get treatment, but he thinks it's not necessary.

Social worker: He thinks it's not necessary….

Mother: Yes that he is recovering, that it was the alcohol and depression that did that, that made him act that way. I tried to explain to him that he needs help….

Social worker: Then what do you think his problem is?

Mother: having had an abusive father who did the same to him

Social worker: yes, his problem is this, his past

Mother: yes, his past that sullies the present

(Isabella, AS Minors Center, 30 years- 3 years work experience)

In initiating this discursive practice, the invitation to present one's point of view is aimed at eliciting from the person the material on which to base a momentary agreement, produce a confirmation of what there is to be said/acted upon, and progressively build up the confirmation of the intervention, then its subsequent reformulation and clarification. The two parties begin to use a common language, and the fact that the mother accepts the problem is a collaborative outcome that depends on the mother, in response to exposing her point of view, offering discursive material that allows a ground for agreement to be circumscribed, so that confirmation of the solution can take place. In conclusion, we can see how in the discursive practices of institutional interaction, built around "viewpoint enactment," participants in the activity are co-implicated in it. In this type of interaction, the social worker is able to do his or her job, that is, to formulate and get an intervention accepted by means of conversation and interaction that incorporates the point of view of the mother and her directly involved partner. In initiating this discursive practice, the invitation to present one's own point of view is aimed at obtaining from the mother the material on which to base a momentary agreement, to produce a confirmation of what the mother herself has understood and said, in order to progressively construct the confirmation of the intervention, its subsequent reformulation and clarification. Thus, it is a process of alignment between the social worker, the mother, and the intervention to be taken. Note also how the effect of this discursive practice is the production of situated social identities. The social worker, in the case above, is not presented as the one whose assessment of the situation is a discovery, nor is the mother constructed as the one who is transported from a state of ignorance to one of knowledge. On the contrary, the interactional work of co-impllication renders the mother as one who knows imperfectly, and the social worker as a professional who in modifying or adding to what the mother already knows and suspects, sets out to ratify and institutionalize the point of view that collaboratively is produced.

Studies on institutional interaction are based on conversational analysis precisely because they are interested in developing comparative studies on institutional discourse. In the above case we can focus mainly on a few elements:

- lexical choices, that is, the way the speaker evokes the institutional context of his or her speech. In fact, when the social worker speaks, as in the story above, he or she refers to himself or herself as an us, since it is the institution that speaks through the individual;
- the organization of the sequences, as we see, question and answer alternate. This is a common sequence in many institutional activities;
- social relations, i.e., asymmetries in institutional interactions, characterize these interactions as opposed to ordinary conversations. Managing asymmetry also involves knowing how to manage the relationship between status/role and discursive rights/duties, constructing "situational identities" that are respectful of the person's dignity. For example, in the relationship between social worker and person, the professional's discursive rights derive from an institutional interaction that strategically directs the discourse. But asymmetry also results from the different distribution of knowledge of the participants in the interaction, and the difference between the

perspective of the institution, which treats the person as a case, and the person who sees his or her case as unique and personal.

We can conclude that institutional interactions constitute an interesting field of study for examining work as a set of discursive practices that allows us to see new things in relation to working through speech.

5.2. Mimetic conversations

Speaking therefore involves a delicate operation of evaluating the situation to choose how to make the word appropriate to the situation, and how to change the situation using the word. Put differently, it involves the realization that context shapes discursive practices, and that these in turn shape context. So let us see how, in work situations, communities of professionals configure and reconfigure their discursive practices depending on the space/time and who is attending the conversation. To illustrate this, we must return to Goffman (1959) and his concept of "spatial regions." To do this we will introduce the case of the "neutral space" of social services that occurs between minor children and noncohabiting parents. Through neutral space we can distinguish the modes of interaction that take place in places and times that are accessible to the sight and ears of professionals (social workers, psychologists, educators, etc.), versus those enacted in more private places and times. Goffman (1959) would use the concepts of stage and backstage. Employing a theatrical metaphor, social life can in fact be viewed in the same way as a stage, on which the actors adhere to what the activity prescribes (and enact a reality that presents no smear to the beholder), as long as they are on stage. Then, when the curtain falls, they move on to criticize, congratulate, and talk to each other in private. Within a neutral space, an ad hoc space is designed to separate front office and back office activities. Architecturally, the neutral space consists of: a waiting room (front office); a meeting room equipped with furniture and games that are adaptable and respectful of each age of the children. It is usually equipped with: a double entrance or division system such that, if necessary, inappropriate, unwanted, or potentially dangerous encounters between parents can be avoided during times of waiting or delay; an outdoor space/small garden; and a one-way mirror or video camera for viewing encounters in another room (back office). The presence/absence of the social worker (or other professionals) changes the discursive relational mode within the household. But it may happen that the nucleus needs to enact private forms of communication even in the presence of the public (waiting room). In analyzing the discursive practice of a team, which is within a neutral space, it is possible to see how working with other colleagues, who in some cases have never been met before, results in a modification of interaction. That is, the team changes its mode of interaction the moment the family group enters the scene. In fact as long as the family unit is in the waiting room, the discursive, ongoing practice of social workers (and other professionals) is turned toward the family group and focused on how they feel, on explaining what is going to happen, and on verbalizing in this way the meaning of what is going to happen. The social worker's behaviors are sensitive and directed toward the presence of the family group until they enter the neutral space. When the family group enters the neutral space, the conversation between the professionals slips to the level of the private, the work to be done, their respective experiences, how they had perceived the attitude of the family group members, the interventions to be envisaged, and so on. Also in the case where there are trainees within the teams of professionals these generally do not get involved in the conversation when the family group is present, whereas when the family group comes in the other experienced professionals also take charge of the training aspect of the trainees, and test them by asking them what they are seeing, what can happen in the performance of this work phase. The team needs to communicate internally in a private form, and needs to discuss and negotiate things that should not be seen or heard precisely by the family group. That is, the team needs to create a backstage within the scene, and at the same time as the action takes place. In this case precisely what Goffman (1959) would call a practice of camouflage takes place, that is, when an activity takes place in the presence of other people. Some aspects of this activity are purposely accentuated, while other aspects, which may discredit their image are suppressed (Hindmarsh and Pilnick, 2002). The team will avoid openly discussing in the presence of the family group its concerns, and avoid asking for clarifications that may cast doubt on their professionalism. Rather, they will create a backstage where they interact nonverbally, using that space in the room that is not visible to the family group, within which they can engage with other professionals. Making use of the space out of the visual reach of the family group.

This example of discursive practice shows how the social worker's workplace is a situational territory, a system of interaction that engages multiple professionals simultaneously in different theaters of actions.

In particular, it makes one reflect on how speech, once it is spoken in such territories, confers the status of a participant in the conversation on everyone within listening range. Discursive practices contribute to forming, spreading and stabilizing a more or less shared understanding of the situation.

5.3. Understanding words

To work therefore also means to enact competent discursive practices, that is, appropriate with respect to the task at hand, the organizational role one intends to play, as well as with respect to the formal and informal rules of the organization where one works, public/private boundaries, and interpersonal relationships with colleagues and other professionals. To describe an example of a collective practice of sense-making, we must refer to what is the definition of sensemaking offered by Taylor and Van Henry (2000) defined as: "an intermediate station on the road to a consensually constructed, coordinated system of action." The intermediate station is the place and time where circumstances are brought together and transformed into a situation that is verbalized, and which can be used as a springboard for intervention. For example, let us analyze the case of a social worker who tells of how a multi-professional team cared for a child whose condition showed signs of violence. In reporting this story we foreground the unfolding of practice leading to understanding of the situation and action. We will include in the story the sequence of moves by which sensemaking is implemented.

> Short Story
> *I had been entrusted with the case of this child who was reported by the school as a missing child case. Following the intervention of social services, during a home visit, I noticed some burns that the child had on his body. I was really worried. Suddenly I remembered seeing some bruises on his body months ago, the day he was wearing a short-sleeved T-shirt for sports. At my questions, the child began to cry. (Antonella, Minors Center, 51 years old- 20 years work experience)*

In work experience, as well as in daily life, we live in an undifferentiated flow of events, akin to chaos. We can imagine how this social worker was doing and thinking a thousand other things until the moment he fixed his attention on those details (bruises and burns). Those details that are noticed interrupt the experiential flow. Just as parentheses, within a sentence, isolate one word or phrase from the others, so the noticed elements are isolated from context. For social workers, this activity should be part of the professional background. In the sense that they represent the activation of knowledge resources that are part of professional competence, experience and perception skills. This knowledge has also been transmitted and taken in the form of mental models and patterns of potential actions, which at the appropriate time interact with the more or less weak signals present in the context. So, sensemaking: (1) introduces order into the flow of events; (2) begins with noticing and isolating. Noticing and isolating a flow of events are activities that rely on the do's and don'ts that Goodwin (1994) "calls professional vision." Indeed, we can imagine that a layman, an outsider to the environment, would never have grasped the importance of those signs and would never have known how to isolate them from context. Nor would he have known how to give them meaning, to give names to what is isolated in the flow of experience. It is practice that organizes individual events in ways that suggest plausible coping, coping activities. These activities are referred to as: "functional deployment." We can see how the social worker moves from noticing signals and isolating them, in the trained awareness that those signals are significant to reporting what she has noticed. Importantly, the social worker refers back to what she had noticed months earlier. That is, she uses retrospective reasoning to identify the situation. That is, items are not discovered immediately, but are created as they are seen, when initial observations are remembered and put together to form a meaningful picture. This makes it possible to identify the subsequent moves of sensemaking: (3) it has to do with labeling; (4) it employs a retrospective personality. Thus, the beginning of the social worker's action is founded on this basis, and the work and interpretive practice continues in the following way:

> Short story
>
> *The thing that had me worried was that those marks--the location of the burn marks for example--could not have been made by the child. His back was full of those round spots. And also the bruises on his arm, you could see they were hands that had been squeezed too hard. It was this set of details that needed to be examined. The placement of those marks on his body. There were a million things that didn't fit.(Antonella, Minors Center, 51 years old- 20 years work experience)*

The interesting thing to note here is that the social worker acts on the basis of her concerns that have become a guess as to what might have happened. This means that further action could test the intuition. But it could also pose a risk to the child. Testing an intuition involves making a conjecture about the nature of the family situation, and progressively testing the initial intuition with successive approximations. Indeed, it is in the method of the social worker's work to proceed by successive approximations, because this activity is subject to risk, to error, and thus requires constant attention to the person and restorative activity (Paget, 1988). It is also a social activity because the social worker's conjecture may be based on various previous factors, on conversations with other professionals, on a casual observation he or she may have made some time ago: a comment heard from a teacher; an interaction with parents, etc. But most importantly, the process of understanding the situation and initiating work practice is distributed, involving the entire office and team. So sensemaking is: (5) the result of conjecture; (6) it is social and distributed. The social worker on the basis of his or her conjectures gradually involves the whole office and the team, sets in motion a plurality of other people from other authorities, other professionals. We can say that the knowledge needed to deal with this emergency is gradually developed. Then the sense of this knowledge is also distributed and is the collective fruit of the process that has been set in motion. This knowledge does not reside only in the head of the social worker. On the contrary, the place where the knowledge necessary and appropriate to the situation resides is not locatable in a defined and uniquely definable place, but is distributed in the team through coordination and more or less weak information among the different professions. Like the psychologist and doctors who can confirm or initiate actions; or a judge who can intervene. It is the more or less persuasive language that activates other knowledge and other people. Acting in this case coincides with speaking, and it is no accident that much of the social worker's practice is acted out conversationally. Knowledge, knowledge in situations, is thus not given but emerges from the coexistence of ignorance and knowledge, through an organizational social practice, which retrospectively attributes order to disorder, and continually looks at disorder in the face of action in the course of action. An activity that may have been appropriate before, that is, looking backward, may become incorrect now. Improvements and deteriorations can take place. All this constitutes situated activity that takes place in and through communication. In communicating by working and in working by communicating it is the speaking that gives existence to events and brings them into being. This is the work of articulation that we described earlier. But to conclude let us see how the social worker is activated in a different strategy.

Short story

Years ago something similar happened to me, I had a similar case. I was beginning to feel like a professional who knows how to do her job but I was not yet able to make my voice heard in the team, the weight of my assessment in such a situation. At that time I went to a colleague who was more experienced than me and asked her to look at my report on that child, and in the process I told her the story. She read everything, talked about the things she thought were relevant with the medical examiner she knew, and immediately he told her to have the hospital examine those signs. The colleague knew exactly what to leverage. (Antonella, Minors Center, 51 years old- 20 years work experience)

This last fragment of the story makes us realize that discursive practices carry with them the whole relational structure of the context in which they are immersed and in which knowing how to speak appropriately to the appropriate person is new. It is knowledge that becomes a resource for action. As much from the individual as from the community that is activated in the course of practical action. In terms of sensemaking this allows us to conclude that it is: (7) the fruit of action; (8) organizing by means of communication. We can conclude by saying that language constitutes an important intermediary in the working practices of the social worker. The use of language in situated communication represents a real activity capable of producing tangible effects. Practical knowledge thus presupposes communicative competence, that is, the knowledge needed to use language appropriately in relation to specific operational contexts. In contemporary society, where social service work embraces many issues, communicative competence is at the very heart of service delivery and the interventions themselves. The social workers we encounter in institutional settings enact discursive practices that produce the service and reproduce the institution to which they belong. Institutional conversations have specific characteristics and in addition to speech make use of artifacts, gestures, predispositions of the environment, enactments from the point of view of the people involved, words and even written documentation. In general, the speaking of work contexts has two distinctive aspects: a subordinate character to the activity; the conversation is open and therefore participation in the conversation is also fluid and open. Discursive practices in workplaces also draw and demarcate spaces of public and private. The respective modes of communication are learned as skills, in saying, silencing and mimicking communication using a code. Working together with other professionals, with judges, presupposes the construction of a common space of mutual understanding and agreement on the methods of understanding. In this sense precisely, we have seen how the concept of sensemaking can be useful in analyzing the practical methods of understanding or misunderstanding, such as working practices and sequences of activities that are not only cognitive. It winds pragmatically through the processes of introducing order into a flow of events, such as noticing, isolating and labeling, employing retrospective rationality. Sensesmaking is then social and distributed, produced in and through action. It is organizing and working through speech. Discursive practices are both functional to the performance of work and symbolic because they make community and indirectly convey deep meanings.

5.4. Using words in writing

Now let us try to understand what actually means working practice in writing, thus distinguishing word from language, that is, the grammatical and syntactic rules that describe and prescribe the correct use of a language. What, then, constitutes competence in the case of language and in the case of speech? A locution may be grammatically and semantically correct, but at the same time it may be inappropriate to the situation and thus demonstrate situational non-competence. As with any discipline and profession, even for the social worker, there are technical terms that constitute the vocabulary of reference in the articulation of a written document. For example, the reports are made up with the threads of professional experience, but each sentence makes contact, ties in with those that have been written before. In addition, the social worker produces documentation that on the one hand is concatenated with methodological and professional aspects, and on the other hand performs administrative functions. The written form enjoys an area of certainty especially in organizationally complex places. Indeed, the written form can be consulted at a distance, it persists in space and time. It acts as a certain point of reference if the correctness or legitimacy of a behavior or the course of an action has to be judged. Technical terms and key words that, Illich (1984) warns in his analysis of languages, have the capacity to mean the same thing in all modern languages, however, risk pushing us toward the illusion that the reality they interpret is basically the same everywhere since they transform different conditions and people into a monotonous uniformity. The philosopher Heidegger (2007, p. 131) stated that: *"it is the word that procures being to the thing,"* and explaining this statement in the words of Vattino (1981), language delimits the field of our possible experience of knowledge. Only through language can things appear to us, and only in the way language lets them appear. The power of speech thus names and establishes worlds within which people, their actions, and their lives are situated, firmly anchoring each signifier to its meaning. This opens up numerous questions with respect to the skills required of social workers to understand the importance and simultaneously the difficulty of documentary action.

> *When I read reports, documents, written mainly by professionals, who use without irony epithets such as "junkies," "old people" or "refugees" or "refugee niggers" sincerely my skin crawls and try to imagine how those who recognize themselves in such epithets might feel: how can they trust those who attribute negative labels to them? (Simona, Reception Center, 31 years old- 8 years work experience). Other times I have read reports where the boy's name was misspelled, or where there were phrases like, "Mom insults her son repeatedly, almost describing a fact without formulating an opinion, changing the reality of the reader. (Simona, Welcome Center, 31 years old- 8 years work experience).*

Words, like any communicative process, not only in social work, are not neutral; they carry enormous weight: the same concept, expressed in different terms, can be offensive or gratifying, can be accepted or repudiated, and so on. They have an influence on those who make decisions, authorize interventions, on those directly affected, and especially on those who become the object of them. Writing, for a social worker, means moving from speech to language, or we might say as Bini (2003) puts it, it means "writing orality." In fact, a large part of writing for the social worker consists precisely in transposing everyday oral communication into written language, in transforming a dialogue into a text, making it become a weave of threads of a fabric. Doing so requires strenuous work, because written language requires planning, building a process that does not allow for excessive digressions and that, once concluded, remains bound by the boundaries established by the writer. And in this way that one's own thoughts, and those of others, are organized into periods, reviewed, analyzed, corrected, interwoven. Writing for a social worker is a process of processing ideas. A transformation of words that belong to the professional and the people who interact with him or her. Therefore, it is important to understand the difference between "how" to write and "what" to write. Goody anthropology (1987) has traditionally focused on the relationships between writing, thinking and social organization. From this field of study has since developed the current that studies ordinary writing and analyzes the pervasiveness of writing in the relational fabric of our society (Fabre, 1997). Within work contexts, the study done by

Narrative

Lacoste called Langage et travail (1994) through which specific writings and products of work practices were studied is important, such as: letters of complaint in public services (Borzeix et al., 1995); maintenance service reports in the IT sector (Fraenkel, 1993); forms in administrations (Pène, 1995). Regarding social service Lanave (2007) explains how writing actually means rewriting, that is, revising, reviewing, and rethinking. Another important effort that it is useful to make is not to conform to styles of "bureaucratese," often making the content incomprehensible and distancing oneself from the recipients of the writings. For that move, erase, retouch and uncover, combine, file revise ideas, perceptions and considerations stopped on paper so that the text reveals them to us and makes their meaning completely obvious.

5.5. Narrative

So far we have talked about the instrumental use of discourse and discursive practices as a work tool and a means of interpreting and constructing the work situation, but we want to expand this view by adding a reflection on narrative as an expression of a collective identity. In recent decades, the strand of studies devoted to narrative, especially of the experience of illness (illness narrative), has seen a proliferation of social studies introducing the discourse on parallel (subjective or group) truths and the (invisible) conflict between different "truths" about illness (Hyden, 1997). Precisely because, as Bruner (1986) argues, narrative knowledge is complementary to paradigmatic knowledge, which is aimed at punctuating the flow of experience, separating and giving comparative evaluations. While the paradigmatic mode allows only one representation of reality at a time, as it is aimed at validation according to a criterion of truth (true/false), the narrative mode allows a plurality of reconstructions at once, all of them plausible. Narrative is to be regarded as a discursive practice that allows the construction of a meaningful link between events or fragments of life that are placed together in a certain order, and that acquire meaning for both the narrator and the listener. It traces an image of weaving between fragments of life, which go on to stitch together a before and an after, the exceptional with the ordinary, attempting to establish explanations, justifications and interpretations of everyday life. Thus, narratives are a way of creating and negotiating meanings and identities (Jedloswki, 2000) and at the same time are an important resource for maintaining, increasing, and disseminating practical knowledge within work groups.

There are numerous studies that analyze narratives within specific communities of practice, such as those of physicians and patients in their various forms, with the aim of relocating the patient and his or her voice within biomedical knowledge. Some of the most famous are the studies of Cassel (1985), Charon (1993) and Brown (1993), whose interest was to study how the patient was "constructed" (defined both symbolically and materially) by medicine and medical practice. These narratives are a tool for understanding the relationship between patient identity and clinical work, a tool for finding better compliance than medical care itself. These situated narratives not only accumulate, preserve and transmit the knowledge of a community, but also celebrate its identity. Knowing community narratives, allows one profession to be distinguished from another, one knowledge from another. And while they specify its identity and strengthen members' belonging and attachment, they also facilitate management and taking charge in multiproblem situations. Stories are often a way to convey specialized knowledge in an indirect form, a message that cannot and will not be conveyed in a direct form. Let us look at an example from this study:

> Short story.
>
> *Within a community for minors, together with the educator I had to determine for the month of June which trips to take outside the center. In fact, the cooperative's contact persons had already decided on the location, the time to spend on the bus, the cost for each individual participant, everything. However, they had neglected to consider the educational goals and had not considered the fact that one of the girls had to complete vocational exams. So I decided to summon the psychologist and pedagogist from the board. As soon as they arrived I tried to tell them the whole story of XXX, so that they would also understand in what particular period these trips would be for the girl. The pedagogist began to expose the educational project to me with data and research in the field trying to argue why that trip organized in that way would be appropriate. I kept telling them that it is not an appropriate trip for the girl knowing her history, her timing and having talked to her about it, and having seen her uncertain and doubtful about going. But I could not find leverage in their thinking. And from there a conflict arose. I asked myself, "How is it possible to integrate and collaborate? To give answers that go in one direction, when in reality we don't even listen to each other among professionals?" In the end, I told them the whole story of xxx, explained everything to them and did it as if I were talking about myself because I knew her so well. Most importantly, I told them what it had meant to me to be the social worker dealing with xxxx. What has been my approach, the method used with her since I first met her. I had never thought so deeply about it. I had never stopped to reflect on my profession. I felt lighter, but also more confident. And finally the*

decision was that we would at least talk to her about it to see what she thought about it. (Antonella, Minors Center, 51 years old- 20 years work experience)

Every story is not subject to a single interpretation, but to many different ones. Its meaning in practice varies according to the point of view of the one who listens to the story and ascribes meaning to it. Bruner (1983) describes the act of understanding a narrative as a "twofold trend": the listener of the story attributes to himself the task of grasping a load-bearing plot in order to be able to understand the meaning of the individual components, but at the same time he is able to extract the plot only from the succession of central elements of which to seek the sequel, and in so doing he defines a plot, which he can share with others. The effect produced by telling a story to other practitioners amounts to sharing the depth of this plot, and the different perspectives, in order to integrate them into one. Telling from a different perspective fosters interconnection among different practitioners, styles, and methodologies. As our interviewee did above, entrusting others with one's experience is very risky and exhausting, but it is possible and useful. This shows how it is possible to construct, through storytelling, work contexts where different representations are shared with common meanings to be relocated in a specific context. Each tells the other what he or she imagines decipherable for the other. It is not a matter of collecting "fragments of truth," but of exchanging meanings and, through the analysis of this exchange, illuminating a shared order. Narratives thus make "community," both for the teller and the listener. And furthermore, paying attention to the stories being told in work practices, being guided by consideration of the symbolic value of those artifacts that allow access to deeper meanings often invisible to some, facilitates the "construction" of a common sense. A kind of new narrative is thus created, a flow that gathers and enhances the voices of all. In short, narratives produce and challenge professional distances, especially when one has to deal with multiproblem situations, and as professionals one entrusts other professionals with something that is deemed con-divisible outside the conceptual domains right-wrong and US-YOU.

Chapter 6

Social workers and the reception of refugees/ asylum seekers: Institutional coordination and cooperation

In this last chapter, in order to analyze the work practice of social workers, we wanted to focus on the institutional coordination that takes place between public agencies, social services and the Third Sector with regard to the reception of refugee/asylum-seeking migrants. This example allows us to reflect on the importance of "working together" for social workers, enabling us to review classic categories of analysis such as cooperation and individual and collective work. This, for social workers, means moving in contexts where there are multiple, sometimes conflicting perspectives. Devising interventions together with the network on the ground involves the challenge of building common ground between actors who often have opposing and different visions (Olivetti Manoukian, 2005). To do this, we used the experience gained during the training of social workers/assistants in the FAMI-ARES project "Actions to strengthen reception services", promoted by the Prefecture of Messina in collaboration with the University of Messina.

6.1. National reception policy framework

Managing reception policies in terms of governance, means acting at the level of a public organization that is always being characterized by the collaboration put in place with other actors from the private and voluntary sectors (Bevirand Rhodes, 2016). Consequently, the reception process fully involves not only state actors, but a heterogeneous universe of organizations and actors collaborating in a multilevel framework. In the Italian system, the main reception tool for asylum seekers and refugees is SPRAR (Protection system for asylum seekers and refugees as well as migrants with humanitarian status), established in the early 2000s and renamed SAI. The latter are set up on a voluntary basis by local authorities who apply in response to notices issued by the Ministry of the Interior, which covers the largest share of costs. The reception facilities, usually managed by local NGOs that participate in local government public tenders, are usually articulated in apartment solutions; include integration measures (legal support, socio-cultural mediation, language learning, support in accessing services and finding work and housing solutions); and are highly regulated and monitored. Since 2014, when there was a sudden increase in mixed inflows, the government adopted a National Plan for the relocation of asylum seekers that authorized Prefectures to establish government reception facilities, called CAS (Centri di Accoglienza Straordinaria) (Extraordinary Reception Centers). Unfortunately, the quality of services provided by CAS has been extremely heterogeneous, with CAS projects ranging from SAI-like solutions organized in apartments and geared toward people's autonomy, to large isolated centers run by for-profit entities and almost devoid of integration services. SAIs represent a clear example of multilevel governance in which both the central government and municipalities are involved, with the latter taking the initiative. In contrast, CAS structures follow a top-down dynamic led by prefectures with little room for maneuver for local governments. The prevalence of CAS over SAI facilities has resulted in a centralization of reception decision-making triggered by the so-called European refugee crisis (Ponzo, Giannetto and Roman, 2022; Caponio and Ponzo, 2022). Within this system, it is primarily social workers who find themselves not only mediating between the culture of the person to be received and the culture of the receiving society, but also having to negotiate between the needs of people and the services offered by the institutions in which they work, at the local level, among various public and non-public actors. The theoretical node we are interested in exploring in this chapter concerns the condition of mutual exchange in situations characterized by the multiplicity of perspectives of those sharing the same work context. There is a need to understand the professional competence of those involved, both because of the inherent complexity of the work practices to be performed, but also because of the difficulties and professional distance between the professionals involved.

6.2. SWOT analysis

During an initial fieldwork phase from September 2022 in the SCIPOG Department premises in Messina, two Project Ares workshops were conducted. The objective was to highlight critical issues in the work practice of social workers in the field of refugee/asylum seeker reception, and possible strategies to be used. An average of 20 practitioners (social workers, operators, educators, etc.) belonging to different agencies/associations in the province of Messina participated in the workshops (Table 6.1).

Table 6.1. Biographical record years profession/service/gender

N° interviews	Name Fantasy	Role	Structure	Age	Gender	Experience
1	Anna	Social Worker	CAS-SPRAR	37	F	10 years
2	Alessio	Social Worker	Welcome Center	32	M	7 years
3	Marta	Social Operator	Welcome Center	41	F	13 years
4	Barbara	Social Worker	Common Social Worker	54	F	27 years
5	Isabella	Social Worker	Minors Center	30	F	3 years
6	Sabrina	Social Worker	Common Social Worker	60	F	37 years
7	Angelo	Social Worker	CAS-SPRAR	46	M	17 years
8	Nino	Social Worker	Minors Center	57	M	27 years
9	Antonella	Social Worker	Minors Center	51	F	20 years
10	Miriam	Educator	Minors Center	38	F	9 years
11	Ernesto	Educator	Minors Center	47	M	11 years
12	Bianca	Social Worker	CAS-SPRAR	29	F	12 years
13	Rita	Social Worker	CAS-SPRAR	27	F	4 years
14	Serena	Social Worker	CAS-SPRAR	28	F	3 years
15	John	Social Worker	USSM-Juvenile Court	58	M	31 years
16	Katia	Social Worker	ASP – Health Services	52	F	23 years
17	Loredana	Social Worker	Common Social Worker	57	F	26 years
18	Elisa	Trainee Social Worker	CAS-SPRAR	22	F	0
19	Simona	Social Worker	Welcome Center	31	F	8 years
20	Mustafa	Mediator	CAS-SPRAR	35	M	5 years

In the first workshop, through a Swot analysis – a strategic planning tool used to assess strengths (Strengths), weaknesses (Weaknesses), opportunities (Opportunities) and threats (Threats) – points emerged that were represented and summarized in these four quadrants:

Strength	Weaknesses
– Knowledge of the territory by the team and professionals	– Failure to comply with the items included in the design
– Frequent interaction with the Prefecture	– Difficult communication between the various professionals involved
Opportunities	**Threats**
– Streamlining administrative procedures	– Employment of some public agencies/officials.
– Improved cooperation among professionals	– Loss of services for refugees/asylum seekers

Combining internal strengths with external SO (Strength-Opportunities) helps us understand that a strength that can be used with opportunities related to the governance process could bring coordination to the prefecture. Furthermore, combining WO (Weaknesses – Opportunities) the strategy to be developed could be the drafting of a memorandum of understanding between all parties involved in order to implement a transformation that can be used to strengthen the hitherto weak elements. Subsequently, in the second workshop, top-down initiatives were analyzed with priority given to the reconstruction of formal lines of authority in service delivery. This allowed the reconstruction of policy making and networks. This part includes the results of the social network analysis developed based on the interactions between actors as they emerged from the survey. Thus, an attempt was made to highlight who were the main stakeholders with whom social workers interact and who, in various capacities, are called upon to cooperate and collaborate to respond to the needs and.

SWOT analysis

Figure 6.1. Reconstruction of policy making and networks

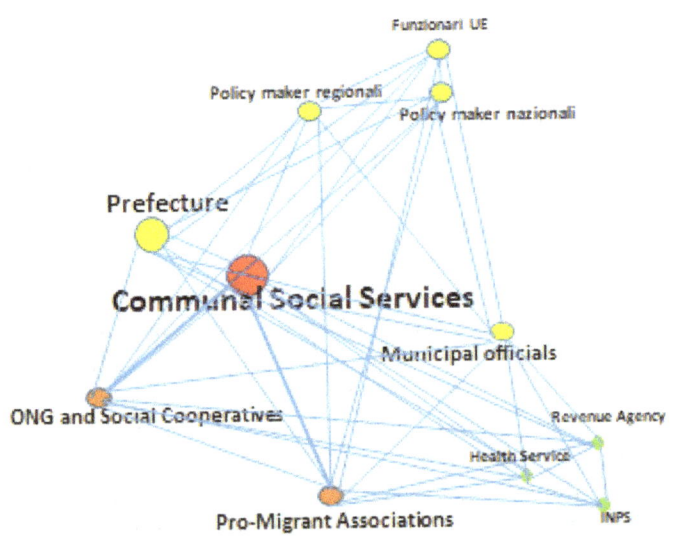

Existing local networks are developed on two different and intertwined spatial levels, namely the municipal and provincial levels, while relations beyond the provincial boundaries are rather scarce. Regional and national policy makers are very peripheral to the network. In fact, EU officials, regional officials, and members of the national government are very peripheral to the network context, confirming the network's predominantly local dimension. In fact, in terms of relations with other levels of government, it should be noted that the most frequent actor mentioned is the Prefecture, while relations with other institutions at the national and European levels is reported as rare. Prefectural policy makers have an important institutional role in implementing reception and integration policies at the local level, being proactive in engaging and promoting local initiatives. Within this framework, the Prefecture has demonstrated the ability to interact with multiple stakeholders, and especially with municipalities, maintaining a central role in reception and integration policy networks. The analysis of social networks suggests that interactions among actors revolve mainly around the Prefecture, municipalities, and NGOs, i.e., local cooperatives operating as providers of reception services, and local pro-migrant associations. Completely absent, on the other hand, are local entrepreneurs, who are difficult to engage, and the same goes for the sparsely existing migrant organizations.

First, it is possible to observe a high degree of coordination between local NGOs and cooperatives and the proactive role played by some municipalities where social services have internal resources for planning. Local NGOs and cooperatives are the most central nodes in the local network. Local policy makers and the administration entrust reception programs to local NGOs and cooperatives, which fulfill several functions: they promote integration initiatives with their own resources; they act as service providers managing public services. Municipal social services, have rather intensive exchanges with local actors regarding reception and integration services, also with a view to regularly monitoring and meeting with private service providers. In fact, the survey-based network analysis shows a high density. However, these exchanges are generally technical rather than political in nature, and often take place through technical tables in order to proceed jointly with planning. Christian and/or left-wing activism, takes key roles in several organizations involved in various capacities in the dynamics of reception. Among these actors, pro-migrant organizations, linked in informal solidarity, play a significant role, through the creation of activities open to the area, examples are public events and courses held; Italian teachers and individual citizens offering their help in various ways; etc. Summing up then, we see a dense network in which NGOs, local cooperatives and municipalities play a crucial role, joined by the Prefecture. In addition, pro-migrant groups are relevant actors. NGOs play a key role, alongside policymakers, in both policy design and implementation of reception and integration measures. Other nodes that have emerged from the network include: refugees/asylum seekers and the National Health Service (in the various ASPs, DSMs, hospitals, and treating physicians); the Internal Revenue Service; and INPS. The functions of these actors involved in the governance of refugee/asylum seeker reception are also analyzed, and more conflict among these actors emerges. Based on the survey analysis, many conflicts are about bureaucracy. Particularly in emergency situations. Becouse they are negatively affected by lengthy regulations and endless waiting times that have made reception and access to services very difficult or nearly impossible.

In light of the data that emerged from the workshops, the triangulation of the information collected in the previous stages was planned, allowing a solid knowledge base and explanatory dimension to be achieved. It was decided to focus, based on the interviews collected (we refer to the part of the introduction for an explanation of the methodology used), on two main themes: (i) attention to cooperation; (ii) situated knowledge and communication between the parties.

For the processing of the material that emerged from the workshops, we identified specific miniaturization tools (Bruschi, 1999) that could hold the acquired text corpus together in an initial summary. It was not easy to govern a text corpus composed of 20 participants and to be able to embrace its salient features at a single glance. In the first stage, thematic summaries were used. The thematic summary summarizes in a few lines the content expressed by all participants, read mainly in light of the questions that inspired this part of research: (i) the focus on cooperation; (ii) situated knowledge and communication between parties. In a second stage, a biographical record was compiled (set taking into account the SWOT scheme, through which the events narrated during the workshops were sorted into a synoptic table describing them, offering for each one three analytical outline information: (a) the educational dimension: years of professional experience; (b) the work dimension: service where the professional activity is carried out; (c) gender. It was thus possible to immediately compare the responses of the 20 participants and, in general, the same textual corpus of interest for the research. The combination of these two stages resulted in a matrix containing some quotations from the workshops, which return some fragments in this direction, and through an analysis of the sequences of the headwords of the interview fragments, taken from the schematization, it was possible to carry out a calculation of the occurrences (most named words) and co-occurrences present in the interviews (Figure 6.2).

Figure 6.2. Thematic clusters (Analysis with TLAB) and recurrent associations of terms

Lemma	Cluster 1	Cluster 2	Cluster 3
Hospitality	10	14	8
Tiredness	10	8	17
Difficulty	11	17	8
Relation	8	10	18
Information	12	14	25
Needs	17	4	7
Bureaucracy	13	11	11
Organization	9	18	9
Service	15	12	14
Suffering	7	18	7

Through the use of TLab software, it was possible to perform a multivariate analysis (Thematic Document Analysis and Identification of Thematic Clusters), which from the calculation of occurrences (most named words) and co-occurrences expressed by workshop participants, allows us to better identify the differential distribution of words and concepts. Thus, it was possible to construct and explore a representation of the corpus content through 3 thematic clusters (semantic areas): Work practice; Cooperation; Communication.

Each cluster results from a set of elementary contexts characterized by the same keyword patterns, and is described through a lexical unit (word-gram) and the variables that most characterize the elementary contexts from which it is composed. The result of the analysis proposes a mapping of general themes characterized by the co-occurrence of semantic traits (Lancia, 2004).

Each cluster is characterized by sets of lexical units that share the same reference contexts, and this makes it possible to reconstruct a thread of discourse within the overall plot constituted by the corpus.

Figure 6.3. Grafh in the X and Y plane

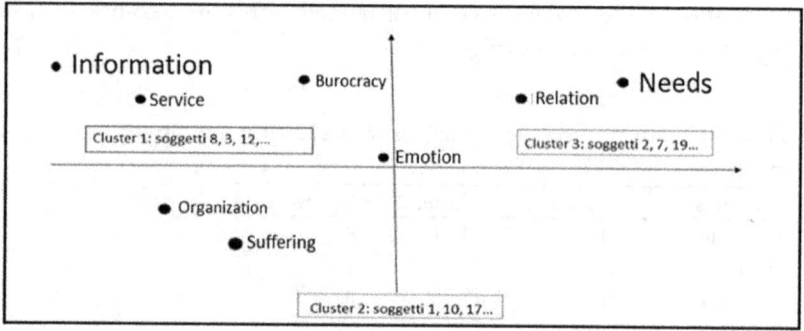

On the first axis, the x-axis axis, is represented the distance between two groups of interviews-Cluster 3 and 1-characterized one by a prevalence of expressions regarding needs, and the other by the prevalence of references to information. The first cluster of narratives is characterized by the noun needs ascribed to the fragile condition of their caregivers, narrated in terms of lack and demands for fulfillment, which the caregivers are advocating for. This word is often associated with the word discomfort, the condition experienced by migrants as experiences related to conquest and confrontation (sometimes even physical) in workplaces, streets, public offices, etc. The second group of narratives (Cluster 3) refers to information, exchange and confrontation with various entities, considered as an important part of professional activity. This inform, is mainly related to the word knowledge, as the skills actually acquired are identified in the circularity of information and the implementation of fluid procedures. These two Clusters are not statistically related to the gender of the teller. On the y-axis, on the other hand, the placement of the narratives with respect to a second element (factor) to which variability is tied, with respect to which a difference is defined (Cluster 2) organizational is graphically represented. In the narratives belonging to Cluster 2, witnesses instead evoke the importance of the organization of the service to which they belong. This system shows how the profession of the social worker is strongly linked to the internal organization of the service/body to which it belongs and the autonomy-decision-making attributed to it. The work dimension therefore seems to have the greatest influence. Finally, the analysis shows that the emphasis on one's professional awareness is predominant in the most experienced people: in these cases it is more difficult to fall into feelings of flattening and feelings of professional discontent. In attempting a more comprehensive interpretation of the variability contained in the workshops conducted, trying to understand how the different themes addressed are associated, it is possible to state that three factors emerge to which to tie the variability contained in participants' responses. The significant incidence of certain characteristics with respect to the use of their words and their association in concepts shows that:

- gender does not influence with respect to the segmentation of one's work;
- the service to which one belongs, or rather the internal organization of the service/body itself, as the type of reading of one's professional activity does not depend on biographical elements, but rather on the ways of recognizing autonomy-decision-making organized internally by the service/body;
- experience, seems to affect more on one's professional awareness, and on the complexity that is determined within the network of cooperation between different services/entities.
- In light of the completed analysis, it is now possible to focus attention on two central aspects that have emerged, namely that relating to cooperation and communication between services/agencies by the social workers working there.

6.3. Attention to cooperation

The social worker working in an SAI works in public, meaning that he or she is always present and, in the face of perturbations and possible ambiguities about the action to be taken, is careful to maintain a firm position. While having to, in many cases, mobilize resources remotely, or make remote placements, the work the social worker does is performed in presence, in close contact with other agencies/Third Sector. The skill the social worker must therefore acquire to do this is based on mutual understanding and the ability to maintain presence. These skills are obviously activated differently in differentiated presence frameworks, depending on the attention the situation requires. In analyzing the interviews, we found three modes of participation, defined as acts of presence, and which we can systematize by linking back to Joseph's (1994) scheme. As people, they are certainly not professionals who function in the manner of "puppets," but we can understand them as cognitive constructs designed to describe an empirical trend.

Short Story 1) Being in the know

One day, while I was on a field trip with the boys, word came from the Prefecture that two refugees/asylum seekers from Mali would be arriving. We were supposed to take them in but, none of the workers were at the headquarters; we were all busy elsewhere. I talked to my colleague who immediately started to get agitated, he couldn't see a solution, who to send, etc. It actually didn't take many to figure out what to do. I immediately talked to the driver and the colleague and explained to them what we were going to do. I remembered that one of our workers was just at the prefecture for a training meeting, and I called her and asked her to meet the two new boys and take all their documentation. And bring them to us at the center. (Simona, Welcome Center, 31 years old- 8 years work experience).

Attention in this case is a mode of presence and participation. Being made aware has the function of calming anxieties and enabling an informed presence about the consistency of the work process and the goals to be achieved. In this case: bringing new kids to the center. Being privy to the overall progress of a team and informed about the collective work constitute a minimal form of active participation.

Short Story 2) Stepping up

I remember the phone call I received from the educator at the center. She was alarmed. I was only a social worker at the time; only a year later I became the director. The director of the center was a sociologist who for reasons of other work was never on the premises. I didn't know what to do. Intervene or leave it until the director intervened? Two boys had just had a fight and were really agitated. There was no way to contain them. They had started throwing chairs and tables out the window. The neighborhood around alarmed had called the police. The educator had locked herself in the office and was afraid to go out, and at the same time she could not open the door to the carabinieri. She could only talk to me on the phone. I had no hesitation, in fact I remembered the balcony that was in the office. I calmed my colleague down and told her that I would go under the balcony of her office and she would have to throw me the keys. When I arrived I saw the neighbors all around, the kids on the balcony screaming, and the carabinieri waiting to intervene. I called my fellow educator barricaded inside who threw me the keys. She immediately opened the door and let them in. As soon as they saw law enforcement coming up the boys calmed down but the same they were caught and taken to the barracks and eventually removed from the center. (Alessio, Reception Center, 28 years old- 3 years work experience)

Situations that break out of normality are those in which the bonds of cooperation within the team change and alter its structure and the frame of participation. It is then that the person appears who exposes himself and takes charge of the situation by managing the urgency, taking responsibility and speaking on behalf of the group. The one who acts as "leader" is someone who is late to the event, in fact she has to resume the course of an affair that occurred in her absence and before her arrival, she supports the people who are in attendance in her place and who alerted her and she needs these to unravel the threads of what is happening. She therefore steps forward, engendering a process that establishes an anticipated certainty in the process of questioning her assigned tasks.

Short story 3) Defile yourself

Several times I have found myself stuck in making a decision. In fact, not all decisions are up to me. There are some choices that have to be made by other agencies, by the Prefecture for example. Or by the courts. I can only follow the progress of events up to a certain point and can only intervene in the ways and times that are my responsibility; other institutions have to do the rest. It is not for me to tell a judge what to do. Residence cards, permits, regulation, employment, and more are issues where I can trigger processes, prepare the way, with my intervention and work, but then it is not for me to decide on the continuation. I wait and assist their decision. And all I can do is trust and almost rely on the other professionals. (Marta, Welcome Center, 41 years old- 13 years work experience).

Defilement is configured as that activity in which one refrains from intervening and relies on what the other person does. One does not pretend to understand something that is part of a system, but waits for the moment of clarification, looks at the autonomy of the other and supports it with a watchful attitude. Indulging and being indulged are the verbs and dynamics of interaction that unfolds in an ever-changing environment where, regardless of hierarchical positions, one is an active or passive subject in a dance of mutual control and cooperation. To defile oneself is not to shirk, but rather to assist, to inform, to utter a word in the working space of other professionals, but without replacing oneself. Thus, it is about being present with one's professionalism and available for collaboration but without having to take an active role in all phases. Thus, we can conclude by saying that working in SAIs means working in physical places in which social workers cooperate to carry out numerous activities with other public agencies/Third Sector. The critical elements of this articulation work (refer to ch. 3.1) are given by time management and the knock-on consequences that an unexpected event can generate. In this sense, the work of the social worker can be considered a model for understanding cooperative work understood as practical knowledge and as situated action aimed at maintaining and reproducing an order. As we have seen in the narratives above, maintaining a distributed and changing structure of attention over the course of the activity is the prevailing pattern of cooperation in the team, but moments of activity complementary to it should also be noted.

6.4. Communication between parties

> *Information is often never given in full and only once. Often you call about something, they answer you and then you find out that something else was missing that needed to be done, but that was not made clear to you, as if they took it for granted. If I ask you for a piece of information I would want it whole, like a prescription, no that later I find out I was wrong for not putting something in and I'm forced to start all over again. You need written protocols, guidelines that should be written together, in synergy.(Simona, Welcome Center, 31 years old- 8 years work experience)*

The use of protocols nowadays has become pervasive because they constitute the idealized image of what one would like to achieve through the dissemination of good practices. In fact, the protocol allows for orderly proceeding and enables one to express agreement on its conduct. It is a kind of guide for attention, intended to instruct one or more practitioners and to enable them to exercise continuous control over the order to be followed, especially when it comes to the priority among things to be done and initiatives to be taken (Joseph, 1994). But how does the adoption of a protocol transform communication between parties?

> *They do not experience the Center. They don't know what happens here. Every day. They don't know all the relational difficulties we have to deal with, and on top of that there are the bureaucratic ones, which make you lose time and patience. On top of that bureaucracy, those people's lives depend and also the investment and sacrifices we have made for them. Seeing documents expire because we cannot communicate with the Prefecture, the Police Headquarters, the Internal Revenue Service...we cannot allow that. Most operators can't tell the difference between a residence permit, they can't decipher it, and as a result they can't determine the expiration date of the health record...and they have no idea what this means for an immigrant. (Alessio, Reception Center, 28 years old- 3 years work experience)*

The possibility to understand, negotiate, support and act lies in situated interaction. However, social workers experience a "physical distance" with the Public Administration, and are forced to channel communication to a mediation (email, phone calls, etc.) that inevitably affects the way in which the interpretative patterns of facts takes place. In many cases this distance leads to an action to be carried out that is constructed differently in the two contexts (Public Administration and Center), and the local knowledge of social workers is not shared and listened to, but remains almost isolated. As Geertz (1983) would say, this local knowledge, which social workers have, or rather contextual and situated, is bounded by experience, and finds it difficult to be shared in those contexts of interaction composed of a plurality of actors and places that however interrelated remain disconnected. Misunderstandings of this kind highlight how the interpretation and choice of action to be carried out interacts with the local context, creating local knowledge that can hardly be shared and communicated. Thus, in contexts where communication is mediated (by telephone, email, etc.) we must emphasize that one of the greatest difficulties lies in the construction of a mental representation of the situation, and in the difficulty of updating this representation when new information is added. In addition, distributed knowledge among all the nodes of the network (public and private social actors) leads to the emergence of situated knowledge that becomes an expression of particular situations and experiences, almost incommunicable. From this we can understand that the action to be performed results from the interaction between the context of the action to be performed and the abstract representation of the action itself, and how communication between these physically distant contexts involves problems whose solution requires crossing the boundaries of the situational knowledge produced.

Considerations

This section highlights similarities and differences among the interviewees and reflects from a comparative perspective on which elements are most relevant in facilitating and/or hindering cooperation, and the importance of communication between the parties. The social workers interviewed have differences, which go to form the basic canvas of this comparative analysis, present scattered and not immediately visible elements of convergence. In attempting a more comprehensive interpretation of the variability contained in the workshops conducted, trying to understand how the different themes addressed are associated, it is possible to say that two factors emerge to which to tie the variability contained. To detect this we focused on the significant incidence of certain characteristics with respect to the use of their words and their association in concepts. The main ones that emerged from the fieldwork are as follows: (a) professional dimension: years of work experience; (b) the work dimension: situated knowledge transfer mode. The path so far task allows us to derive some relevant elements in order to understand the mechanisms that can influence the social worker's work practice, without claiming to highlight empirical regularities on the basis of which to build generalizations: Social workers who have more than 10 years of work experience considers cooperative work as practical knowledge and as situated action aimed at maintaining and reproducing an order, which allows the professional to be present with his or her professionalism and available for cooperation with other professionals, without having to take an active role at all stages and without feeling the need to replace other professionals. Years of professional experience therefore show a significant connection with attitudes of cooperation toward other professionals. In fact, in professionals with less work experience the focus on cooperation and appears reduced.

(A) work experience positively influences cooperation. Social workers who have more than 10 years of work experience consider cooperative work as practical knowledge and situated action aimed at maintaining and reproducing an order, which allows the professional to be present with their professionalism and available for cooperation with other professionals, without having to take an active role at all stages and without feeling the need to replace other professionals. Years of professional experience therefore show a significant connection with attitudes of cooperation toward other professionals. In fact, in professionals with less work experience, the focus on cooperation appears reduced.

(B) On the other hand, with regard to communication between parties in contexts where communication is mediated (by telephone, email, etc.) it is shown that one of the greatest difficulties lies in the construction of a mental representation of the situation, and the difficulty of updating this representation when new information is added. In addition, distributed knowledge among all the nodes of the network (public and private social actors) results in the emergence of situated knowledge that becomes an expression of particular situations and experiences, almost incommunicable.

We can therefore conclude this paper by stating that in delving into the analysis of social workers' work practice as processes in which they enact their practical knowledge necessary to accomplish their work, the basic assumptions to be considered are:

– The work of the social worker is a practical activity constructed by both the social worker and others (people, professionals, technicians, etc.), within situations and interactions that take place predominantly face-to-face, and therefore need to be studied in situ;
– Cooperation and communication in practice, with the rest of the team, is the result of the continuous adjustment of contingencies that emerge from context and situated knowledge.

From the research some of the aspects of the social worker's work that have long remained in the shadows are brought to light when studying this profession as a practical cognitive activity through a revitalisation of micro-sociological studies.

It emerges how the specificity of the social workers' activity should lead to a review of the difficulties of training, not only initial university/academic training, but above all ongoing training, related to the management of increasingly complex problems, and which should be further stimulated with valid incentives. As Riva (2009) would say, in fact, the development of social workers' professionalism is related to the dissemination of knowledge acquired through training. This awareness is most evident in professional social workers who emphasise how training can determine not only the achievement of a balance in the concrete relationship with their profession, but also the acquisition and reworking of an awareness, a reflective capacity, and a work practice that is built over time with experience. The professional identity of social workers is not a stable entity, but is a continuous process of interpretation and personalisation, of reflection. In this sense, it should be seen as the continuous path of reflexive growth that runs through the different stages of initial and continuing training, and that allows the professional to change, modify, bind and experiment with all the different forms of his or her knowledge. Will we see in the coming years a revisiting of the professional practice of social workers?

Bibliography

Abbott, A. (1995). Boundaries of social work or social work of boundaries? Social Service Review, 69, pp. 545–562.

Archer, M.S. (2003). Structure, agency and the internal conversation. Cambridge University Press.

Archer, M. S. (2012). The reflexive imperative in late modernity. Cambridge University Press.

Barber, B. (1963). Some problems in the sociology of professions. Daedalus, XCII, pp. 669–688.

Bartholini, I. (2016). Identità di genere e habitus professionale dell'assistente sociale. In I. Bartholini, R.T. Di Rosa., G. Gucciardo, F. Rizzuto(Eds.), Genere e servizio sociale. Napoli: Edizione Scientifiche e Artistiche.

Becker, H.S. (1962). The nature of a profession. In Education for the professions, yearbook of the national society for the study of education, pp: 27–46.

Benner, P. (Ed.) (1994). Interpretive phenomenology: Embodiment, caring, and ethics in health and illness. Thousand Oaks, CA: Sage Publications.

Bevir, M., Rhodes R.A.W. (2016). Rethinking governance: Ruling, rationalities and resistance. London: Routledge.

Bini, L. (2003). Documentazione e servizio sociale. Manuale di scrittura per operatori. Roma: Carocci.

Blumer, H. (1962). Society as simboli interaction. In A.M. Rose (ed.), Human behaviour and social processes. Boston, MA: Houghton Mifflin.

Borgatti, S.P., Halgin, D.S. (2011). On network theory. Organization Science, pp. 1–14.

Borzeix, A, Fisher, S., Fornei, M., Lacoste, M. (1995). La lettre de reclamation. In L'administration de l'équipement et ses usagers, a cura di Quin C. Paris: La documentation Francaise, pp. 71–107.

Bourdieu, P. (1979). La distinction. Paris: Critique sociale du Jugement, Minuit.

Bourdieu, P. (1990). Le sense pratique. Paris: Edition de Minuit.

Boutang, Y.M. (2002). L'età del capitalismo cognitivo. Innovazione, proprietà e cooperazione delle moltitudini. Verona: Ombre corte.

Boutet, J., Gardin, B. (2001). Une linguistique du travail, Vol. 2001. Borzeix e Fraenkel, pp. 89–112.

Boutet, J., Maingueneau, D. (2005). Sociolinguistique et analyse de discours: facon de dire, facon de faire. Langage et société, n. 114, pp. 15–47.

Brown, P. (1993). Psychiatric intake as a mystery story. Culture, Medicine and Psychiatric, 17, pp. 255–280.

Bruner, J. (1983). In search of mind. New York: Harper&Row.

Bruner, J. (1986). Actual mind, possible words. Cambridge, London: Haward University Press.

Bruschi, A. (1999). Metodologie delle scienze sociali. Milano: Mondadori.

Campanini, A. (1999). Servizio sociali e sociologia: storia di un dialogo. In M. Dal Pra Ponticelli (a cura di), Lineamenti di servizio sociale. Trieste: LINT.

Carbone, S. (2022). La costruzione dell'identità professionale degli assistenti sociali tra percorsi di formazione e rielaborazione. *La rivista di servizio sociale*, II, pp. 29–41.

Cardano, M. (2011). La ricerca qualitativa. Milano: Il Mulino.

Cassel, E.J. (1985). Talking with patients, Vol. 1. Cambridge: MIT Press.

Castells, M. (1996). The rise of the nerwork society, Blackwell, Oxford; trad. it. La nascita della società in rete. Milano: Egea, 2002.

Charon, R. (1993). Medical interpretation: Implication of literary theory of narrative for clinical work. Journal of Narrative and Life History, 3, pp. 79–97.

Conein, B., Jacobin, E. (1994). Action situéè et cognition: le savoir en place. Sociologie du travail, 94, pp. 475–500.

Corbin, J., Strauss, A. (1993). The articulation of work through interaction. Sociological Quarterly, n. 1, pp. 71–83.

Dal Pra Ponticelli, M.(2005). Prendersi cura e lavoro di cura. Padova: Fondazione Emanuela Zancan.

Demazière, D., Dubar, C. (2000). Dentro le storie. Analizzare le interviste biografiche, trad. it. Milano: Raffaello Cortina.

Dent, M., Whitehead, S. (2002). Managing professional identities: Knowledge, performativities and the 'New' professional. London: Routledge.

Bibliography

Di Rosa, R.T., Gui, L. (2021). Cura, relazione, professione: questioni di genere nel servizio sociale. Milano: Franco Angeli.

Donati, P. (1983). Introduzione alla sociologia relazionale. Milano Franco Angeli.

Donati, P. (2006). Perché il paradigma relazionale nell scienze sociali? Da dove viene e dove porta? In I. Colozzi (ed.), Il paradigma relazionale nelle scienze sociali: le prospettive sociologiche. Bologna: Il Mulino.

Drew, P., Heritage, J. (1992). Analyzing talk at work: An introduction. In P. Drew, J. Heritage (a cura di) Talk at work. Cambridge: Cambridge University Press, pp. 3–65.

Engeström, Y. (2008). From team to knot: Activity-theoretical studies of collaboration and learning at work. Cambridge University Press.

Fabre, D. (1997). Par écrit: ethonologie des écritures quotidiennes. Paris: Edition dela MSH.

Fargion, S. (2005). Le nuove linee di tendenza nell'organizzazione dei servizi sociali e la professione di assistente sociale. Dal Pra Ponticelli, (a cura di), Prendersi cura e lavoro di cura. Padova: Fondazione Emanuela Zancan.

Fargion, S. (2013). Il metodo nel servizio sociale. Riflessioni, casi, ricerche. Roma: Carocci.

Fargion, S. (2021). Il percorso di crescita della professione come pratica e come disciplina. La rivista di servizio sociale, 61, n. 1, pp. 4–7. https://doi.org/10.1400/285659

Ferrario, F. (2004). Le dimensioni dell'intervento sociale. Un modello unitario centrato sul compito. Roma: Carocci.

Ferrarotti, F. (1969). Il ruolo del servizio sociale nella società italiana contemporanea. Quaderni della rivista di servizio sociale, n. 7.

Ferruta, A. (2000). Un lavoro terapeutico. L'infermiere in psichiatria, Milano: Franco Angeli.

Flexner, A. (1915). Is social work a profession?. School and Society, XXVI, pp. 901–911.

Florea, A. (1966). L'assistente sociale: analisi di una professione. Roma: ISTISS.

Folgheraiter, F. (1998). Teoria e metodologia del servizio sociale. La prospettiva di rete. Milano: Franco Angeli.

Folgheraiter, F. (2001). Fondamenti di metodologia relazionale. La logica sociale dell'aiuto. Trento: Erickson.

Folgheraiter, F. (2009). Saggi di welfare. Qualità delle relazioni e servizi sociali. Trento: Erickson.

Fraenkel, B. (1993). Pratique d'ecriture en milieu hospitalier: le partage de l'enonciation dans les ecrits de travail. Cahiers langage et travail, n. 5.

Freidson, E. (2002). La dominanza medica. Le basi sociali della malattia e delle istituzioni sanitarie. Milano: Franco Angeli.

Garfinkel, H. (1967). Studies in ethnomethodology. Englewood Cliffs: Prentice Hall.

Geertz, C. (1983). Local knowledge. New York: Basic Book.

Gherardi, S. (1990). Le micro-decisioni nelle organizzazioni. Bologna: Il Mulino.

Gherardi, S. (2006). Organizational knowledge: The texture of workplace learning. Oxford: Blackwell.

Gibbons, S.B. (2011). Understanding empathy as a complex construct: A review of the literature. Clinical Social Work Journal, 39, n. 3, pp. 243–252. https://doi.org/10.1007/s10615-010-0305-2

Giddens, A. (1994). Le conseguenze della modernità. Fiducia, rischio, sicurezza e pericolo. Bologna: Il Mulino.

Glaser, B., Strauss, A. (1967). The discovery of grounded theory: Strategies for qualitative research, trad. it. Roma: Armando Editore.

Goffman, E. (1956). Encounters. New York: Macmillan; trad. it. Espressione ed identità. Bologna: Il Mulino, 2003.

Goffman, E. (1959). The presentation of self in everyday life. New York: Anchor Books.

Goffman, E. (1961). Asylums. Essays on the social situation of mental patients and other inmates. New York: Anchor Books, Doubleday & Company, Inc.

Goffman, E. (1967). Interaction ritual: Essays on face-to-face behavior. New York: Anchor Books.

Goode, W.J. (1957). Community within a community: The professions. American Sociological Review, XXII, pp. 194–200.

Goody, J. (1987). The interface between the written and the oral. Cambridge: Cambridge University Press.

Goodwin, C. (1994). Professional vision. America Anthropologist, n. 3 pp. 606–633.

Goodwin, C. (2000). Practices of seeing. Visual analysis: an ethomethodological approach. In T. Van Leeuweven, C. Jewitt (a cura di) Hanbook of visual analysis. London: Sage, pp. 157–182.

Goodwin, A.M., Gore, V. (2000). Managing the stresses of nursing people with severe and enduring mental illness: A psychodynamic observation study of a long stay psychiatric ward. British Journal of Medical Psychology, 73, n. 3, 311–416.

Granovetter, M. (1973). The strength of weak ties. American Journal of Sociology, 78, pp. 1360–1380.

Granovetter, M. (2012). Interview with Mark Granovetter: «Organization theory and economic sociology go along side by side». Journal of Economic Sociology, National Research University Higher School of Economics, 13, n. 3, pp. 8–21.

Greenwood, E. (1957). Attributes of a profession. Social Work, II, pp. 44–55.

Grosejan, M., Lacoste, M. (1999). Communication et intelligence collective. Le travail à l'hopital. Paris: Puf.

Gumperz, J.J. (1989). Engager la conversation. Introduction à la sociolinguistique interactionnelle. Paris: Edition de Minuit.

Heidegger, M. (2007). In cammino verso il Linguaggio, trad. it. di A. Caracciolo e M. Caracciolo Perotti. Milano: Mursia.

Hindmarsh, J., Pilnick, A. (2002). The tacit order of teamwork: collaboration and embodied conduct in anesthesia. The Sociological Quarterly, n. 43, pp. 139–164.

Hughes, E.C. (1958). Men and their work. Glencoe Il: The Free Press.

Hyden, L.C. (1997). Illness and narrative. Sociology of Health, pp. 48–69.

Illich, I. (1984). Il genere e il sesso. Per una critica storica dell'uguaglianza. Neri Pozza.

Jedlowski, P. (2000). Storie comuni. Mondadori: Milano.

Johnson, T. (1972). Professions and power. London: Macmillan.

Joseph, I. (1994). Attention distribuée et attention focalisée. Les protocols de la cooperation au PCC de la ligne A du Rer. Sociologie du Travail, n. 4, pp. 563–585.

Lacoste, M. (1994). Langage et travail: quelques perspectives. Sociologie du travail, Année, pp. 45–56.

Lanica, F. (2004). Strumenti per l'analisi dei testi. Introduzione all'uso di T. Lab. Milano: Franco Angeli.

Laneve, C. (2007). La trama oltre il filo. La riscrittura come sorpresa. Demetrio.

Lave, J. (1988). Cognition in practice. Cambridge: Cambridge University Press.

López-Pastor, V., Monjas, R., Manrique, J.C. (2011). Fifteen years of action research as professional development: Seeking more collaborative, useful and democratic systems for teachers. Educational Action Research, 19, pp. 153–170. https://doi.org/10.1080/09650792.2011.569190

Mead, G.H. (1934). Mind, self and society. Chicago Il: University of Chicago Press.

Merleau-Pounty, M. (1945). Phenomenologie de la perception. Paris: Gallimard; trad. it Fenomenologia della percezione. Il Milano: Saggiatore, 1965.

Moore, W.E. (1970). The professions. Roles and rules. New York: Russell Sage Foundation.

Neve, E. (2008). Il servizio sociale. Fondamenti e cultura di una professione (2nd ed.). Roma: Carocci.

Numerato, D. et al. (2012). The impact of management on medical professionalism: A review. Sociology of Health and Illness, 34, pp. 626–44. https://doi.org/10.1111/j.1467-9566.2011.01393.x

Olivetti Manoukian, F. (2005). Per una nuova progettualità del lavoro sociale, Vol. 2005. Animazione sociale, gennaio, pp. 26–59

Paget, M. (1988). The unit of mistakes. Philadelphia: Temple University Press.

Parsons, T. (1939). The professions and social structure. Social Forces, XVII, pp: 457–467.

Pene, S. (1995). Traces des mains sur le ecrit gris, in Paroles au travail, a cura di Boutet J. L'Harmattan, pp. 103–122.

Pickard, S. (2009). The professionalization of general practitioners with a special interest: Rationalization, restratification and governmentality. Sociology, 43, n. 2, 250–67.

Polany, M. (1958). Personal knowledge. Toward a post-critical philosophy. Chicago Il: University of Chicago Press; tard. It. La conoscenza personale. Verso una filosofia post critica. Milano: Risconi, 1990.

Pontecorvo, C., Ajello, A.M., Zucchermaglio, C. (1995). I contesti sociali dell'apprendimento. Milano: Led.

Ponzo, I., Giannetto, L., Roman, E. (2022). The key roles of policy legacy, politics and civil society. InT. Caponio, I. Ponzo, (eds.), Coping with migrants and refugees. London: Routledge.

Prandstraller, G.P. (1999). Dalla sociologia delle professioni all'analisi dei gruppi professionali. Conversazione con Federico Butera e Gian paolo Prandstraller. In M. Giannini, E. Minardi I gruppi professionali, Sociologia del lavoro, pp. 70–71.

Ridley, M. (2003). Nature via nurture: Genes, experience, and what makes us human. New York: HarperCollins Publishers.

Riva, V. (2009). Riflessività: il contributo della sociologia per il servizio sociale. La Rivista di Servizio Sociale, n 3.

Ruggeri, F. (2013). Stato sociale, assistenza, cittadinanza. Sulla centralità del servizio sociale. Milano: Franco Angeli.

Saunders, C. (1955). Metropolitan condition and traditional profession relationships. In R.M. Fischer (a cura di). The metropolis in modern life. New York: Doubleday.

Schegloff, E.A. (1986). The routine as achievement. Human Studies, n. 9, pp. 111–151.

Schön, D.A. (1983). The reflexive practitioner. New York: Basic Books (trad. It. Il professionista riflessivo, Dedalo, Bari, 1993).

Schon, D.A. (1983). The reflective practitioner: How professionals think in action. New York: Basic Books.

Schutz, A. (1979). Saggi sociologici. Torino: Utet.

Sicora, A. (2005). L'assistente sociale riflessivo. Lecce: Pensa Multimedia.

Simmel, G. (1908). Soziologie. Untersuchungen uber die former der vegesellshaftung; trad. It. Milano: Sociologia. Comunità, 1989.

Strati, A. (2004). L'analisi organizzaztiva. Roma: Paradigmi e metodi. Carocci.

Suchman, L. (1987). Plans and situated action: The problem of human-machine communication. Cambridge: Cambridge University Press.

Taylor, J.R., Van Henry, E.J. (2000). The emergent organization: Communication as its site and surface. Hillsdale: Lawrence Erbaum.

Tousijn, W. (1994). Il sistema delle occupazioni sanitarie. Processi di professionalizzazione e dominanza medica. Polis, 8, n. 2, pp. 203–222.

Tousijn, W. (2008). L'autonomia professionale di fronte alla sfida consumerista e alla sfida manageriale. In L. Speranza, W. Tousijn, G. Vicarelli (eds.), Vol. 2008, pp. 73–92.

Vattimo, G. (1989). Essere, storia e linguaggio in Heidegger. Genova: Marietti.

Wilensky, H. (1964). The professionalization of everyone?. American Journal of Sociology, 70, n. 2 pp. 137–158.

Winograd, T., Flores, F. (1986). Understanding computers and cognition: A new foundation for design. Norwood: Ablex.

Witz, A. (1992). Professions and patriarchi. New York: Routledge.

"Work & Society"

The series "Work & Society" analyses the development of employment and social policies, as well as the strategies of the different social actors, both at national and European levels. It puts forward a multi-disciplinary approach – political, sociological, economic, legal and historical – in a bid for dialogue and complementarity.

The series is not confined to the social field *stricto sensu*, but also aims to illustrate the indirect social impacts of economic and monetary policies. It endeavours to clarify social developments, from a comparative and a historical perspective, thus portraying the process of convergence and divergence in the diverse national societal contexts. The manner in which European integration impacts on employment and social policies constitutes the backbone of the analyses.

Series Editor: Philippe Pochet, General Director ETUI-REHS (Brussels) and Digest Editor of the Journal of European Social Policy

Published books

No 88 — *Knowledge and practical knowledge. For an analysis of the working practices of social workers*, Silvia Carbone, 2024, ISBN 978-3-0343-4930-7

No 87 — *Christian Democracy and Labour after World War II.* Cecilia Maria Bravi, Andrea Maria Locatelli (eds.), 2023, ISBN 978-2-87574-596-5

No 86 — *Trade unions in the European Union. Picking up the pieces of the neoliberal challenge.* Jeremy Waddington, Torsten Müller and Kurt Vandaele (eds.), 2023, ISBN 978-2-87574-634-4

No 85 — *Les défis de la diversité culturelle dans le monde du travail au XXIe siècle. Politiques, pratiques et représentations en Europe et dans les Amériques,* Ariane Le Moing, Saïd Ouaked et Christèle Le Bihan (dir.), 2020, ISBN 978-2-8076-1082-8

No.84 — *Austerity and the Implementation of the Europe 2020 Strategy. Reshaping the European Productive and Social Model: a Reflexion from the South,* Javier Ramos Díaz and Esther Del Campo (eds.), 2017, ISBN 978- 2-8076-0436-0

No.83 — *The New Pension Mix in Europe Recent Reforms, their Distributional Effects and Political Dynamics*, David Natali (ed.), 2017, ISBN 978-2- 8076-0265-6

N° 82 — *Accompagner vers l'emploi. Quand les dispositifs publics se mettent en action*, Christèle Meilland et François Sarfati (dir.), 2015, ISBN 978-2- 87574-352-7

N° 81 — *Outiller les parcours professionnels. Quand les dispositifs publics se mettent en action*, Sophie Bernard, Dominique Méda, Michèle Tallard (dir.), 2016, ISBN 978-2-87574-351-0

N° 80 — *Politiques de la diversité. Sociologie des discriminations et des politiques antidiscriminatoires au travail*, Milena Doytcheva, 2015, ISBN 978-2- 87574-290-2

No.79 — *Activation Policies for the Unemployed, the Right to Work and the Duty to Work*, Elise Dermine, Daniel Dumont (eds.), 2014, ISBN 978-2- 87574-232-2

No.78 — *The Transnationalisation of Collective Bargaining. Approaches of European Trade Unions*, Vera Glassner, 2014, ISBN 978-2-87574-167-7

N° 77 — *L'Europe entre marché et égalité. La politique européenne d'égalité entre les femmes et les hommes, de l'émergence au démantèlement*, Sophie Jacquot, 2014, ISBN 978-2-87574-159-2

N° 76 — *Représenter le patronat européen. Formes d'organisation patronale et modes d'action européenne*, Hélène Michel (dir.), 2013, ISBN 978-2- 87574-057-1

No.75 — *The Wage under Attack. Employment Policies in Europe*, Bernadette Clasquin & Bernard Friot (eds.), 2013, ISBN 978-2-87574-029-8

No.74 — *Quality of Employment in Europe. Legal and Normative Perspectives*, Silvia Borelli & Pascale Vielle (eds.), 2012, ISBN 978-90-5201-888-1

No.73 — *Renewing Democratic Deliberation in Europe. The Challenge of Social and Civil Dialogue*, Jean De Munck, Claude Didry, Isabelle Ferreras & Annette Jobert (eds.), 2012, ISBN 978-90-5201-875-1

No.72 — *Democracy and Capabilities for Voice. Welfare, Work and Public Deliberation in Europe*, Ota De Leonardis & Serafino Negrelli (eds.), 2012, ISBN 978-90-5201-867-6

N° 71 — *Trajectoires des modèles nationaux. État, démocratie et travail en France et en Allemagne*, Michèle Dupré, Olivier Giraud et Michel Lallement (dir.), 2012, ISBN 978-90-5201-863-8

No.70 — *Precarious Employment in Perspective. Old and New Challenges to Working Conditions in Sweden*, Annette Thörnquist & Åsa-Karin Engstrand (eds.), 2011, ISBN 978-90-5201-730-3

No.69 — *Europe 2020: Towards a More Social EU?*, Eric Marlier and David Natali (eds.), with Rudi Van Dam, 2010, ISBN 978-90-5201-688-7

No.68 — *Generations at Work and Social Cohesion in Europe*, Patricia Vendramin (ed.), 2009, ISBN 978-90-5201-647-4

No.67 — *Quality of Work in the European Union. Concept, Data and Debates from a Transnational Perspective*, Ana M. Guillén and Svenn-Åge Dahl (eds.), 2009, ISBN 978-90-5201-577-4

No.66 — *Emerging Systems of Work and Welfare*, Pertti Koistinen, Lilja Mósesdóttir & Amparo Serrano Pascual (eds.), 2009, ISBN 978-90-5201- 549-1

No.65 — *Building Anticipation of Restructuring in Europe*, Marie-Ange Moreau (ed.), in collaboration with Serafino Negrelli & Philippe Pochet, 2009, ISBN 978-90-5201-486-9

No.64 — *Pensions in Europe, European Pensions. The Evolution of Pension Policy at National and Supranational Level*, David Natali, 2008, ISBN 978-90- 5201-460-9

No.63 — *Building Anticipation of Restructuring in Europe*, Marie-Ange Moreau (ed.), 2008, ISBN 978-90-5201-456-2

No.62 — *Jobs on the Move. An Analytical Approach to 'Relocation' and its Impact on Employment*, Béla Galgóczi, Maarten Keune & Andrew Watt (eds.), 2008, ISBN 978-90-5201-448-7

N° 61 — *Les nouveaux cadres du dialogue social. Europe et territoires*, Annette Jobert (dir.), 2008, ISBN 978-90-5201-444-9

No.60 — *Transnational Labour Regulation. A Case Study of Temporary Agency Work*, Kerstin Ahlberg, Brian Bercusson, Niklas Bruun, Haris Kountouros, Christophe Vigneau & Loredana Zappalà, 2008, ISBN 978-90-5201- 417-3

No.59 — *Changing Liaisons. The Dynamics of Social Partnership in 20*th *Century West-European Democracies*, Karel Davids, Greta Devos & Patrick Pasture (eds.), 2007, ISBN 978-90-5201-365-7.

No.58 — *Work and Social Inequalities in Health in Europe*, Ingvar Lundberg, Tomas Hemmingsson & Christer Hogstedt (eds.), SALTSA, 2007, ISBN 978-90-5201-372-5.

www.peterlang.com